BODYBUILDING MIND

Think and Grow Muscle with Mental Training

Paul M Maher PhD

This edition published in 2023
by DreamEngine Media

978-1-915212-10-8

Email: publishing@dreamengine.co.uk
Website: DreamEngine.co.uk
Social Media: @DreamEngineuk

Other Books by the Author
Cricket Mind
Bodybuilding Mind
Tennis Mind

About the Author
Paul M Maher PhD

Paul has had a lifetime of experience in the Health & Fitness industry; beginning as a trainer, then gym manager and sports therapist which ultimately led him into sports psychology. His enthusiasm and success made it a natural progression to create a series of sports psychology books to guide athletes in mind control to improve their performance. The techniques in these sports' psychology books are designed to give the athletes the tools to help themselves.

Look out for more books in the The Mental Game series.

The Mental Game is a series of books written for athletes who wish to tap into the power within their mind and gain an edge on the competition. The books include techniques to improve performance, assert focus and control when under pressure and gain a precious edge on the competition.

The author, Dr Paul Maher, began work in the health and fitness industry during the 1980s as a trainer, then gym manager before becoming a sports therapist. Following fifteen years as a clinical hypnotherapist, he studied for his PhD in Sports Psychology and began writing on the subject in 2011.

Today, performance enhancement needs psychology, whatever your sport. These books teach methods which can lead to significant improvements. Practical, do-it-yourself, user-friendly instructions are clearly explained step-by-step. Just read through to understand your mind, set goals, control anger, gain belief, master emotions and gain that precious advantage.

These books are a toolbox for winning The Mental Game. When you need to tackle a problem, you can quickly find the appropriate strategy; read as much as you need or use it as a refresher. Not only will these books help you directly improve at your sport, but they are also packed with fascinating knowledge and skills you can apply in your whole life.

To win the game, first you must win The Mental Game

ATTENTION

The information presented here is intended for people in good health, The ideas, suggestions and techniques are not a substitute for proper medical advice. Anyone with medical problems of any kind should consult a medical practitioner. The author does not prescribe any technique as a form of treatment for any physical or mental problem. Any application of the ideas, suggestions or techniques given here are at the readers sole discretion.

This publication contains the authors opinion in the subject matter covered herein. The intent of the author is to offer information to help you in your efforts to improve your bodybuilding, so makes no warranty of any kind for any particular purpose. If you use any of the information in this publication for yourself or others, neither the author nor the publisher is liable or responsible to any person or entity for any consequential, incidental or special damage caused or alleged to be caused directly or indirectly for the information contained within.

TABLE OF CONTENTS

FOREWORD

I have always had an involvement in fitness, beginning with simple exercise when I was at school. After leaving school I went to sea in the 1970s and represented the ships I served on at soccer, cricket, hockey and swimming. I later began my career in the Health & Fitness Industry after studying Physical Culture in the 1980s and became a gym manager in Gibraltar. Returning to the UK after a spell in Greece, I became a REPS Level Three Exercise Professional and expanded into Sports Therapy where I worked in several private, independent gyms.

With further study, I extended my qualifications by becoming a Clinical Hypnotherapist and finally gained a PhD in Sports Psychology after eight long years. I have spent a fair amount of time learning and understanding how the mental side of sports affects performance and most certainly, enjoyment.

This book is written for Bodybuilders and Figure Competitors at all levels as a practical guide to help them train consistently with excellence. My research has found very little on mental skills training for bodybuilders. Most professionals, followed by an increasing number of amateurs, now understand how to improve their training, belief, motivation, posing confidence and master their emotions with mental training. However, I have yet to meet any bodybuilder who fully appreciates all of his or her psychological strengths or weaknesses.

My purpose is to teach you how to change the way you think and give you the tools to achieve your ambitions and reach your full potential, if that is what you truly desire. The secret to success lies in controlling your thoughts. The techniques described here come from Sports Psycholgy, Neuro Linguistic Programming (NLP) along with ideas from my own clinical experience in Sports Hypnosis.

When you become successful, you will feel good about yourself, what you do and what you have. Then your life becomes a better place to be.

Love your Bodybuilding.

Paul M Maher PhD

INTRODUCTION

*"You have to train your mind like
you train your body."*
Bruce Jenner

Welcome. I want to share with you techniques that will motivate you toward success. Teach you mental training strategies that have helped many bodybuilders break through sticking points and control your thinking, so you can have the body others only dream of having.

Throw away any limitations forever and catapult yourself to new heights. It will not take you long to read this book, but the techniques you learn will serve you in your bodybuilding career and in your life. Bodybuilding can be a life-long occupation, you may as well have the best one.

Close your eyes for a moment and really think about the most fantastic life you can imagine. Step into amazing levels of success, an extraordinary muscled body with biceps, pecs, thighs of your dreams, whatever that dream may look like for you. Gaining awards in Bodybuilding and in your personal life. Picture yourself basking in the vision. Run your hands over favorite muscles. Relish the feeling of knowing you will always have your health and fitness.

Eyes open now. That's the dream. What does your reality look like? Do the two match up? Is it everything you desire? Maybe you started out a few years ago with big goals and even bigger dreams but now motivation has slowed down. Are your workouts harder, but you no longer see results? Are you looking for ways to set yourself apart from your competition? Do you want to take yourself to the next level but worry you don't have what it takes?

You can turn your wildest dreams into reality, attract all you most want out of life, overcome fear of failure, disappointment, hardship and struggle. By taking responsibility, you build your dreams from the inside. By creating a winning picture of yourself using the well-tested techniques here, you can inspire confidence within yourself and create a clear, strong, unmovable certainty your life will never be the same. Taking responsibility puts you in the driving seat. You no longer have time to blame others or be a victim of events or circumstances. You create the events and circumstances to get the most rewarding life you ever dreamed possible.

Let me answer the question going on in your mind – what's it all about? Mental skills and sports psychology are not modern concepts, they have been around for as long as sports have been played and are as much about mental attitude as solid technique. An athlete can conquer or remove a variety of issues they would normally struggle with and help them shape and expand their psychological and behavioral qualities, which will also improve their physical capabilities.

If you are cynical, believe learning is boring, or think this is all new-age fluff, we need to have a chat. It does work. Hundreds of therapists like myself and thousands of clients say it does work. There are poor therapists about, so if you or a colleague have tried something like this before and failed, get over it! Sorry to be so blunt, but naysayers will never become better bodybuilders.

As a human, you have an incredible mind that can sometimes get wired up in a way that is not useful for some of the situations you find yourself in. Your subconscious mind acts in a literal, even naive way. As it's non-judgmental, it will readily absorb a bad idea as much as a good one. Culture, family, peer pressure, a bad coach, all teach ways that sometimes just are not useful for what you want to achieve and can crush your dreams.

This book is just like having me sit down with you and go over, step-by-step, exactly how you do the techniques. The goal of this book is to help you get greater control of yourself by planting positive suggestions in your mind. The secret to successful bodybuilding is very simple as I have said, take responsibility and do something – anything at all! Even if you mess up, you will be wiser for the experience. You have to take action.

Read this book from cover to cover, then read it again. Make it an ongoing journey. The more you can digest this information, the more it will have an impact on you. All of these techniques need to be practiced. Find ten minutes every day to work on any you find interesting and beneficial. Use the book as an interactive tool to challenge, excite, inspire and teach. Don't underestimate the methods, you will find them invaluable. If you consider a technique you find strange or not to your liking, simply find another you can adjust to suit your needs, there will be one that may excite you on another page.

Allow yourself some quiet space and time to go through these techniques properly. It can all start with one technique and it will start by knowing that technique well. Don't attempt to go all out to learn them all right away.

Learn one then extend your range, just as you would developing a particular body part.

I have made examples of bodybuilding situations, but you are free to use them as a template which can be adopted to suit your needs. They are not quick-fix cures, you have to put the time in to learn how to use them, but the successful strategies you are about to learn will help you begin making a wave of changes, now, on this first day. Chances are you will be bitten by the bug as you find your confidence grow. Excited? You should be. These methods can rock you to your core. As a bonus these methods can also affect other areas of your life. Just sit back, put your feet up and enjoy what I am going to teach you.

It starts here.

FOR PERSONAL TRAINERS

"Expect to be observed."
Vince Lombardi

Getting the best from your clients is one of the greatest skills required by any personal trainer. How well you communicate depends on your clients response, which means you are responsible for how they understand you. Pay attention to the words you use as your words can open up the possibility for change in them. Have a look toward the end of the *Motivation* chapter for more use on using words.

The techniques here can help you to motivate and encourage your clients. Please note, mental skills training is something you DO with your client, not TO your client. If you use any of the methods in this book on any of your clients, there are a number of steps to use for best results:

Before attempting a technique, you must know if it is absolutely right to correct your clients thinking. Are there any negative consequences? You must be sure there will only be good, ethical consequences to come from making any change to their attitude. This is best established by asking these questions:

What is the purpose of this change?
What will the client gain or lose by it?
What will happen if they make the change?
What will not happen if the client does not make the change?

Explain the process to your client.
Establish where your client is with their particular mental attitude and where they would like to be. This is best provided by asking them where they think they are using the benchmark of 0 – 10, with 0 being no problem at all and 10 being very high. For example, if you have a lady who is concerned she will turn into a muscular giant within a few weeks of using weights, 0 would be nothing to worry about while at the other end, 10 would be extremely anxious.

Use one of the techniques, when complete apply the 0 – 10 benchmark scale to find out if your lady client's anxiety has reduced.

If appropriate, you could ask your client to imagine a future situation which previously would have created their issue and notice how they feel about it now. Repeat this as often as you feel is needed until your client is convinced their attitude has changed for the best. Pay attention to any non-verbal communication your client is showing. Is their voice tone and body language in accord with their verbal responses?

Be aware some clients may have repressed or traumatic memories which are beyond your ability to change and may be best dealt with by a qualified therapist. Some techniques are surprisingly powerful and can have a greater impact on your client than you may realize. Is there a history of mental illness or depression in their family? Is your client on medication? Does your client have a history of epilepsy? If in doubt, DO NOT work with them.

I have often heard a personal trainer tell a client when something is wrong, then give misleading advice on how to correct it, besides inventing all kinds of theories. Even comments to clients like "you're not trying hard enough," place the client on a long, lonely road. Encourage clients without getting too technical or theoretical. You must know your stuff, but don't blast the client with your knowledge unless asked.

At the heart of mastery to be a personal trainer are qualities of leadership, confidence, knowledge and empathy. Competent personal trainers have a great influence on the lives of their clients. They are masters at communication. They support their clients and challenge them to grow and become the best they can be in a positive and respectful manner.

Do you understand yourself...

WHAT ABOUT YOU?

"Be yourself, everyone else is already taken."
Oscar Wilde

Your behavior is a result of your self-image - the person you believe you really are. Your self-image is so strong your behavior will have you perform consistently as the person you think you are.

We all know people who are quite muscular, yet they think they are not. They think they have arms that are too fat, or legs which are too skinny, they feel too old or too out of shape. Human stories with faces, names and voices full of hopes and fears, aspirations and anguish. If you believe yourself not good enough in any way, you will subconsciously sabotage any efforts to make yourself a winner.

Studies have proven, time after time, an amazing amount of sportspeople in general fail because they think themselves less than they are worth by this limited self-image. Are they unworthy? Of course not. It's how they see themselves in their imagination which affects their sport performance and can even cause self-destructive behaviors.

Here's an example to prove my point. Sit for a moment somewhere quiet and remember a time in the past when you felt tired, sad, or despondent. Really get back to that time by remembering everything you could see and hear in as much detail as you can. Bring back any physical or emotional experiences, get hold of that memory and keep it in mind for a few seconds. Try to stand up.

Sit down again and this time bring back to mind a time when you felt energetic, determined, optimistic. Again remember in as much vivid detail as you possibly can what you saw, hear the good sounds you heard and get in touch with the physical and emotional sensations you had then and hold them all in mind for a few seconds. Now stand up.

Compare those two experiences. In the first you may have found it an effort to stand. How about the second? Did you leap up ready to go? Your thoughts influence how you perform. Isn't it interesting that in just a few seconds, thinking one way then another, created an entirely different result. Your belief about yourself influences your thoughts, which then affect your behavior, as this book will prove.

That said, let me remind you how quickly your bodybuilding career goes by. For instance, it's incredible how quickly the last twelve months have gone by. How was it? Think about your own mortality a moment. Imagine your breathing your last. Did you see and do all you wanted to do in bodybuilding? Did you truly live it? Train as often as you wanted? Enjoy wonderful moments with training partners? Try out new routines?

Before you know it, you find yourself retired, then into old age and there you are, staring at Father Time while reflecting on how good you could have been. That's how it ends for the vast majority of people. Where did all the time go?

The only thing you have total control of in this world is your thinking. At first, you may feel self-conscious trying out these methods. Whenever you do something new that takes you beyond your comfort zone you feel some nerves. It's OK, you're human! Grit your teeth and get out of your comfort zone. Be task-conscious not self-conscious.

So, do you have an in-depth understanding of yourself? Do you recognize and value your temperament and character? Be careful, people often see only what they want to see when it comes to self-evaluation. Self-understanding will influence your bodybuilding career.

Calm people are not affected emotionally by success or failure as much as excitable people. Being calm makes it easier to concentrate, however being more laid-back may make someone react slower to negative situations.

Excitable people are almost always on the go and are at risk of reacting too emotionally. These people also use up a lot of time and energy by being so intense.

Ask three or four friends or training colleagues you can trust to grade their impressions of you. What would they say your mental strengths are? Your best psychological abilities? Include attributes such as attitude, competitiveness, confidence and persistence. Spend some time reflecting on what they said. Do you agree?

This book will present you with methods you need to do to develop the future you want. Nothing in your life is going to change unless you change. If you decide to take the wisdom outlined on these pages, you will understand you are fully capable of mental and physical feats. You are bigger than you think, capable of more than you can imagine.

You are now in the process of thinking with belief...

BELIEF

"Man is what he believes."

Anton Chekhov

Belief dominates your behavior whether positively or negatively and behavior affects your performance. Your physical behavior is controlled by belief. A belief is knowing with absolute certainty what something means. That belief can mean the difference between a recreational trainer and a world conqueror. You may have the genes and the talent to become a great bodybuilder, yet if you do not believe that 100% you will struggle. Success or failure – you always prove yourself right! That recreational trainer can improve with the desire belief can bring.

In other ways, belief can determine your quality of happiness, health, wealth and success. It even has a greater influence on your life then the actual truth.

Notice the successful bodybuilders. They have made more mistakes than those who haven't tried. Every mistake has been accepted as a learning opportunity. They were never discouraged by failure. They continued to believe in themselves. Just believe in yourself also. Failure is part of the learning process not the end of it. It is only a frustration.

When have you failed? Only when you stopped believing. Every response was information to tell you what actions were getting you closer to, or further away from what you wanted.

We all get stuck in our beliefs however sensible we think they are. You may find it interesting that you tend to believe what you think is true without question. If you believe you can't get ripped, it's that you believe you can't, but the interesting thing is, if you tell yourself you can get ripped, that gives you permission to question that old belief and soon you will find, with correct training and attitude, you can get ripped, can't you? What you believe isn't necessary real, you just have to invest in yourself. Confused? The nice thing about being confused is you come away with something new.

Seriously challenge yourself about the training you cannot improve on. Can you learn something else? Is there a method you have not yet developed? Belief creates self-talk – how you speak to yourself inside your head. If you are going to say something to yourself, you may as well make it something encouraging.

Mental blocks are often difficult to deal with as they involve changing a belief regarding what you can or cannot do. When there is a mental block, sometimes there is something going on in your personal life affecting how you see things. Are you bottling up any feelings?

> *Take a belief which is holding you back.*
> *Think about, or write down, what it's opposite, more positive belief is.*
> *Imagine what it would be like living this new belief.*
> *Believe that:*
> *You do have the ability to succeed.*
> *You can accomplish what you set your mind on.*
> *There are no problems, just opportunities.*
> *You are creating your future now.*
> *If you can believe you are destined to be bodybuilder, you will be.*

So you see, just because you believe something, it does not necessarily mean it's true. You can reconsider your beliefs and decide which are useful to yourself and worth maintaining and those negative beliefs which you now know can be changed. A beneficial belief change you can make here and now is that you can master the techniques outlined in this book, very easily and quickly.

Now that kind of thinking can give you a buzz you won't believe!

Believe in the power of your imagination...

IMAGINATION

Henry Ford

Imagine I've just cut a lemon in two and I've handed you one of the halves. Feel it's texture there in your hand as you bring it up to your mouth. Be aware of the citric smell when you place the juicy fruit in your mouth. Now suck on all that tangy lemon juice and feel it run down your throat.

As you're reading this, imagine both of your hands are submerged in a bucket of hot, soapy water. You can remember what that's like? Did you have a bath last night? Wash the windows, or even your car? Recall that feeling of hot, soapy water on your hands, make it vivid, feel those pinpricks of watery heat.

Your subconscious mind does not recognize fact from fiction. A real or imagined event. It's just like a DVD recorder. It records sights and sounds continuously. Your body then treats every vivid thought and image as if it were real. Ever awakened from a nightmare? Notice how your body responds to the vivid use of your imagination more so than from a conscious command. If you order your heart to speed up, it probably won't. If you imagine in detail walking down a dark, sinister alley late at night and hear fast, approaching footsteps behind you, I bet your heart beat will increase. What about that nightmare? It wasn't real, but you woke up in a sweat, your heart pounding, gripped by fear and it took a while for you to calm down.

Everyone has the ability to imagine. I may have just proven it to you. If not, answer these questions:

Think of your locker in your changing room. What does it look like? Which side does the door open on? What sound does it make when you shut it? To answer those questions, you had to use your imagination.

By changing the pictures and sounds in your mind, you can gain conscious control of any aspect of your sport. Using images of yourself that are bigger, brighter and bolder, have a greater impact than those that are smaller, duller or further away. Let me show you.

Think of someone you find stressful in the gym to be near or compete against. Think about facing them again. A bad memory can hurt you like a knife. Here is something you're going to love. Recall their face. As you do so, ask yourself:

Is their memory in color or black & white?
Is their face in your memory to the left, to the right, high or low, or right in front of you?
Is their face in your memory large or small?
Is it light or dark?
Moving or still?
Are their any voices, any sounds?

Now play around with the way you remember that person. Make each of the following changes in turn and notice what happens:

If the memory has color, drain it all away until it is like a black & white photo.
Move the location of their face and push it further away from you.
Shrink it down in size.
Turn down the brightness, make it blurry.
If the image was moving, freeze frame it.
What sound do you hear? Is it their voice? Change it by giving them a squeaky voice like a cartoon character, or a deep, sexy one, go on, do it.

Give the face a clown's nose, bright orange or green hair. Mickey Mouse ears. Go on, have fun!

Altering your memory can change how you feel. Think of that person now in this new way. How do you feel? Probably the stressful memory has reduced if not gone completely. Not only do you feel different now, the next time you see that person, imagine how much more comfortable you will feel. You control your emotions, not someone else controlling them.

***

Let me show you how to use your imagination in a way known as *association and dissociation.*

Think of another stressful or uncomfortable memory. Keep that image in your mind, now imagine you can step out, away from yourself so you can see the back of your head. You may be skeptical, at least give me a hearing. Now move away as far from the situation as you can. Step all the way out of the picture so you can still see it, but way over there somewhere as if it is happening to someone else. Shrink the picture down. Lose all the color. Turn the background fuzzy or white. Fade away any sound. Notice by dissociating reduces the intensity of the feeling you were having. It takes courage to learn new skills such as these.

You can do similar to heighten a good memory, by association. When you think about happy memories, you re-create the happy feelings associated with them.

Remember a time when you felt really confident, aware of your ability, strength and self-belief. Let that image come into your mind, make it juicy. Step into that memory as if you were there again, seeing through your own eyes, hearing through your ears and feeling how successful you felt in your body. Expand the memory, make it bigger, brighter, the feelings stronger, turn up the sounds and make them richer. If you can't remember a time, imagine how it would feel to be totally confident . You get what you focus on.

To reduce a negative memory, step out, move away from it (dissociate). Watch it as if it's happening to somcone else. Shrink it, take away the color, turn it dull, out of focus. Make the sounds quieter, further away. Doing this can make any bad emotional response drain away. Notice you are controlling how it affects you.

To improve a positive memory, zoom in and fully experience it (associate). Make the image bigger and closer, intensify the color, increase the brightness, make the sounds closer, clearer, louder – unless it is a memory of peace and quiet. Live it. You can have a great deal of fun with these methods.

***

Imagine you are on the stage, posing. Step into a picture of yourself in control, moving to the rhythm of the music. Feel mighty and proud. Hear the applause from the audience. Make it louder. See the standing ovation, the approving looks from the judges.

Visualize winning a trophy and holding it up. Feel it's weight, the touch of cold metal. See from your mind's eye, out. Now see from the audiences perspective. See from the judges view. Picture yourself on the stage standing apart from the other competitors, holding the trophy up, see the picture from different angles. Now go back inside yourself and see from your own eyes, hear from your own ears. A champion wins in the mind first.

You can use your imagination to free yourself of any old, negative beliefs that might be limiting yourself. Imagine them written or painted on a wall. Gripping a huge hammer like a strongman, attack the wall, demolish it completely, see the dust, hear the clattering of the bricks as they tumble. Feel the energy you are using until the words or images are totally destroyed.

You could imagine them written or drawn on paper. Feel the paper between your hands as you rip it to shreds, hear it, feel it, see it happen there in your mind's eye. Finish off by ritually burning the paper. I said some methods would challenge you – this is all revolutionary stuff!

Here's an easier one. Close your eyes and imagine in your mind a picture of you with the body you wish to have. Notice how you look, your stance, the expression on your face, all the tiny details. Take that picture and throw it up into the air and multiply it so that hundreds of copies come raining down all around you as far as your eyes can see. They even go into your past and future.

Did that feel awkward? Exercises like these may seem silly at first but while you control the pictures in your mind and how they sound, your not at the mercy of anyone else or circumstances and they direct your subconscious mind toward having the body you want. Transform your mind – you will transform your body. A flame will ignite inside you.

It will boost your confidence...

CONFIDENCE

"Building character takes discipline."
Vince Lombardi

Finishing the season with a trophy can give your efforts a huge boost. The one key toward bodybuilding success however, is confidence. The more confident you are, the more effectively you will train.

Confidence makes you look like you mean business. It is the intent you are giving out so it is important for you to be aware of self-confidence in yourself as a person, be it dependability toward commitment, integrity, honesty, sincerity, your values and the various roles you play in your life, along with your training confidence.

Let's see if you can develop more confidence. On a piece of paper make two columns where you are going to write down all your essential elements toward bodybuilding. Make a heading on the first column entitled *practical skills* where you put your fitness, strength, flexibility, diet, gains and all the physical stuff and in the second column *interpersonal skills* as here you will list things like assertiveness, communication, confidence, resilience.

Come back to this list on a regular basis as further realizations come to you. Get some feedback from trainers or friends who's opinion you can trust. Write down everything no matter how insignificant you may at first think it is, especially in column two as here you will find an indirect, but noteworthy influence on your bodybuilding career.

When the list is finally complete, rate yourself on each aspect you have written down out of ten. Be honest. Resist the urge to rate yourself as much as you would like. Show the list to colleagues or your trainer and compare how they would rate you out of ten. Scores that are markedly different are worth reflecting upon.

***

Here is another exercise worth spending some time on. The instructions are easy to follow. List four or five of your best training sessions and remember as much detail about them as you can. Allow your mind to remember the sights, sounds, smells and feelings you had before, during and after each successful workout. Really think about these sessions in detail and notice how your confident feelings begin to increase.

Self-confidence is based upon realistic self-perception that will lead to an overwhelming desire to make quality judgments to be the best you can.

You can make things happen with ego-strengthening...

EGO-STRENGTHENING

"The harder you work, the harder it is to surrender."
Vince Lombardi

If you truly want to be victorious you must be active, not passive. The approach toward ego-strengthening is in the development of your positive inner resources which have come from your positive experiences, including emotions from self-worth, confidence and pride that you feel inside of yourself for your efforts in bodybuilding and in your life.

Ego-strengthening is important so that, as the optimistic bodybuilder that you are becoming, you have the inner confidence to strive for achievement along with an increased arousal and focus. There is always something new to learn, examine or develop.

A method you can use to demonstrate the power of your positive talk is through *muscle testing*. What you do here is create a specific target you would like to reach, let's say a new bench press weight. With the help of a training partner, stand while you hold out an arm horizontal to the side, at shoulder height and as rigid as possible.

Placing one hand on your shoulder, your partner will then test to see how much exertion is required to push your arm down about six inches while you resist. This is to make a base measurement of your strength. Your partner will then make a series of tests following a verbal statement from you.

First think and say aloud "I don't know whether I will be able to bench press 180 lbs but I hope I can," or whatever the target weight you have set is. Your partner then apples force to your arm again and notes how much strength is required to bring it down six inches.

Next, you will think and say aloud "I will try to bench press 180 lbs," while your partner again pushes your arm down to determine if more or less force is required then the first test.

Lastly, you will say aloud and believe "I will bench press 180 lbs," while your partner tests your arm strength again.

The test will prove to you that by first doubting, then believing, as the sentence becomes more positive each time, will produce a stronger arm than the previous test and you and your partner should feel the increased strength as the statements become more positive.

Negative beliefs that do not support you can be buried in your subconscious mind. By muscle testing, it becomes available for you to find those inner resources you possess, then something unusual, but enlightening will occur for you to create lasting change.

To help increase your ego-strengthening, decent challenging and appropriate goal setting should not be ignored, along with positive visualization exercises you will learn throughout this book.

Next, I'll teach you about self-talk...

SELF-TALK

Also known as internal dialogue, self-talk is simply the way you talk to yourself inside your head. You worry if you will stop gaining muscle, congratulate yourself after a hard training session, even tell yourself how sexy you look in fresh, clean, training kit. People do it every day, but mostly it's negative. Blaming yourself, chastising yourself, "I'm not fit enough," "I'm too tired," "I'm not able." This low energy talk is a major cause of poor motivation. If you tell yourself something often enough, you will begin to believe it. It may not be true, but you will certainly believe it is.

High-energy words promote high-energy thoughts and unlike low energy words, you can practice using high-energy words until your thoughts and emotions adjust for the better. Then your training session becomes a positive, high-energy experience.

If you have negative beliefs, you have negative self-talk, which will confirm the negative belief and so it goes on. You must be aware of your internal dialogue. If the voice you use is not supporting you in any way, change it. While positive thinking may not always work, negative thinking almost always does. Put aside the self-pity and accept the responsibility to change.

Dwelling over poor memories leads to negative self-talk along with emotional discomfort. Your mind then remembers similar bad situations. Allowing the past to affect you instead of focusing on the present only slows you down. You suffer tight muscles, energy loss, poor co-ordination, leading to loss of lifting style, then you risk injury. Future chapters will show you the techniques to use to get over these poor memories.

Be good to yourself when you talk to yourself by talking positively. Make mental pictures of yourself being a total success. See yourself lifting heavier, hear the congratulations of your spotter or training partner and the applause from spectators at competitions and feel how good you feel when you practice being a winner. Mental rehearsal is the next best thing to actually being successful, so do it as often as you can and review it, including positive self-talk. You will be delighted when you see those improvements.

What do you say to yourself when things go wrong? What do you say to yourself when confronted by a challenge?

The secret is a confident bodybuilder will talk differently than one who lacks that confidence, even though they train similarly. Training and performing with confidence gives you the security to enjoy every minute and will be reflected by your gains. Without that confidence, someone else may always feel unprepared, nervous, undecided. Those thoughts will then reinforce those beliefs. So you can understand how vital confident, positive self-talk is.

Research shows three or four positive thoughts to every negative one contributes to better performance. Your words can literally become your world. Keep track of both the positive and negative thoughts you have about yourself so you can change any negative thinking.

Making positive affirmations will help you feel more confident, but to work effectively these affirmations need to be practical and inspiring. Boastful declarations become banana skins as they do not work in the real world and are fruitless distractions.

Are you holding yourself back through perfectionism...

PERFECTIONISM

Perfectionists can get hung up on themselves doing everything perfectly! They can be their own worst enemies because they are never satisfied. A self-critical perfectionist can never be perfect in their mind because of a fear of making mistakes. This is their greatest barrier to success. Perfectionism damages excellence. Perfectionism does not exist, excellence does. Beneath the desire to succeed and reach excellence, a perfectionist often has an ultra-negative, condemning voice going on inside their head.

Yes, a perfectionist hates to lose, but a perfectionist must not get anxious about losing.

For some, their belief is anything less than perfect is unacceptable. Even when gains are being made they are unable to feel any real fulfillment, as in their eyes, they never do anything of sufficient standard to warrant feelings of personal satisfaction.

Many psychologists believe perfectionists have turned out that way due to conditional parenting. Their child's role in life has already been decided by them. Rarely satisfied parents want their child to achieve more then they did and who desire their offspring to be a sporting success have no idea what they are doing to their child's self-esteem with their critical ways. When they criticize, they are telling their child, or so the child believes, s/he is a failure in their parents eyes. Children are easily influenced and will develop that fear of failure in their subconscious which can affect them for years to come.

Children coming from a volatile, neglected family life may think that doing everything to perfection will get them reward, recognition and help them gain control of their unstable environment.

Although not a psychiatric illness, mental health can sometimes be affected. Anorexia, obsessive compulsive disorder, social anxiety or depression can stem from a darker form of perfectionism. Sufferers are unlikely to seek help as, being perfect, they do not recognize they have any problem.

So, when you do well, do you give yourself enough credit? When you do poorly, do you beat yourself up? Do you punish yourself when you make mistakes? If you gang up on yourself there are now two people fighting you. All bodybuilders experience failure at some stage, it's how you emotionally handle it that determines if you leave it in the past or re-create it over and over.

Focus on the things you can control. Put errors behind you, loosen the chains on your self-criticism – let it go! Don't get angry with yourself, move on. Concentrate on what is happening in front of you, in the present, forget what has happened, it's history.

Perfect bodybuilders are optimistic, do you think they criticize themselves...

THE INNER CRITIC

Everybody is a critic and the worst you will ever come across is the one inside your head. This talk has a damaging affect on your emotional state, far worse than someone in the gym screaming at you. What does it sound like? Is it angry, sarcastic, resigned? When you make a mistake I'll bet you never say "good, that's another learning experience."

People think because there is a voice inside their head, they must listen to it. You can choose.

It is important to analyze what you do in bodybuilding, but only relative to the situation. Your criticism should be constructive feedback if it's going to be of any use. If your critical self-talk is not supporting you, play with the direction and tone of the voice you hear. Like many of the methods presented in this book, this one may seem strange at first. Go give it a shot, you have nothing to loose and everything to gain if it works for you. Is that reasonable?

You feel lethargic, you don't gain muscle, you berate yourself for missing training. Notice your critical voice using that nasty tone.

Now notice from where it is coming from. Is it inside or outside your head? From the front, sides, or back?

If your right handed, extend your left arm, left handed, extend your right.

Wherever the critical voice came from, imagine you can move it away from your head to your shoulder, then to your elbow, down to your wrist. Now move it all the way down to the tip of your thumb.

Hear the voice repeat the same statement, only this time as if you hear the voice coming from the tip of your thumb. Slow it right down or speed it up. Change it to something comical like Mickey Mouse, Donald Duck or another cartoon character.

You can move the voice down to your big toe.

You can use another voice to make the critical one shut up.

This technique can also be used on a bad memory of someone talking critically at you. You understand this?

I'll make an interesting comment about critical self-talk. It always takes hold in the subconscious as a command. So if you tell yourself you are not going to manage another rep, or make no more gains, then it will probably happen. This is because negative self-talk generally has a strong emotion attached to it. A positive suggestion, no matter how good the intention, is usually wishful thinking, it does not contain that emotional content.

If you want to change for the better, pay close attention to the words you use on yourself.

Power, timing and good lifting style can get gains working and when you repeat positive words with enough emotion, you start to believe it. Use words and phrases that will motivate you and fill you with enthusiasm for the sport. Every bodybuilder has two competing voices, one is a negative critic, the other a positive coach. Who you listen to is your choice.

Let's re-program your self-image...

RE-PROGRAM
YOUR SELF-IMAGE

Goethe

To alter any poor memories or attitudes you may have, first weaken them, then create better alternatives by using the methods outlined in this book. You will be better able to go into activities and situations with an abundance of vigor and enthusiasm. Just give yourself time.

Clasp your hands in your usual way, fingers entwined and notice which thumb is on top. Let go then clasp your hands again in such a way as the opposite thumb is now on top. How does that feel? Awkward? Uncomfortable?It does not feel natural! The further you go into unfamiliar territory, the greater the psychological discomfort.

Change does that. If you were to place your hands and thumbs in the awkward position every time, it would eventually feel natural.

Can you adjust to a high intensity training routine, or a new fat-burning session? This next method will teach you how you can create a sense of self-mastery:

Take a deep breath and relax as you exhale.

Tighten, then relax all your muscle groups.

Recall the sights, sounds, feelings of when you exercised at your very best.

In your minds eye imagine another you standing in front of you. This is the best 'you' you have ever been, or ever will be. At the top of your game.

If you can't see it or imagine it, just know that it is there.

When you feel happy with the image in front of you, notice the way you stand, move, lift, contract your muscles.

Notice a confident champion – you, standing in front of you.

Now step into your image and see through those eyes, hear through those ears, feel how good it feels to be that living image.

Keep those important feelings and make everything bigger, brighter, more powerful. Let it glow.

You can step into another, more intense image of yourself. Do it several times, getting bigger and bolder and stronger each time.

Take a few minutes if you wish, to imagine yourself in any situation from the past where you want a bad memory changed to a more positive outcome, or see yourself in a future situation, dominating the gym by your very presence, being rewarded, applauded, excelling. You can, you know, forget about ever having that bad memory. Daydream and know it can come true.

Think of a future situation or event when having a positive feeling will be desired. You have read the routine, give it a go, or try this one next.

***

Using the *Circle of Excellence* exercise builds a positive mood and creates a state of mind which will be useful in the future:

In front of you, create a Circle of Excellence. This represents the state you require. Imagine it has a color, maybe there is a sound there or a special motivating word. This circle brings for you all the positive assurances you want.

Return to a time when you had a positive resource or imagine you had the attitude, dedication and grit.

Choose a special motivating word that will have meaning for you, or a sound.

Take a deep breath, exhale.

Step into the memory inside that circle. Hear that special sound or word, imagine the feelings you have getting stronger, being absorbed by your body. Strength and enthusiasm glows from you. Your more tenacious, confident, fitter. Every breath you take, you take in more of these resources. Imagine the bright color shinning down and all around going into every cell of your body, from the top of your head, all the way down to the tips of your toes. Double it.

Tell yourself you are more talented, confident, fitter.

If you can see it in your mind's eye you can achieve it.

Imagine that feeling you have getting stronger, being absorbed by your body. Strength and enthusiasm glows from you. You're more tenacious, robust, committed.

You can do the Circle of Excellence just about anywhere. Rehearse first, then going into the gym, imagine the circle before you just over the threshold. Do it as you take position at a machine, before you squat, before you dead lift or any other exercise. How about stepping out of the shower, getting out of a car. You're re-creating that super body.

Feeling good? Your learning to master your emotions...

MASTER YOUR EMOTIONS

You keep coming back for more now, don't you! Any unpleasant thought you have comes with an unpleasant feeling. If you want to win the game going on inside your head, you have to deal with your emotions. I'm going to guide you to be your most confident self and feel resourceful in just a moment, for any endeavor you choose.

You may encounter a broad range of emotions naturally before, during and after a workout. By being aware and monitoring your emotions you can become aware of your optimal performance state.

You may be wondering, what is an emotion? An emotion is the mood you are in at any particular moment and is individual and unique to all of us. Love, hate, confidence, fear, they are all emotions and we constantly go in and out of them all day long. All behavior is the result of an emotion.

Remember times when you were filled with confidence, determination, joy, optimism. How about that passion you feel for bodybuilding? Unfortunately you also suffered anger, guilt and resentment. Emotions are your subconscious mind's way of telling you there is something going on you need to pay attention to.

It's useful to take a brief look at emotions for you to gain more insight. A primary emotion occurs closely to the event that brings it on, so it is the emotion you feel first. A secondary emotion appears after the primary emotion. You could feel joy as a primary emotion, that will then lead to bliss or delight, pride or optimism.

Sometimes the problem with primary emotions is that they disappear as fast as they arrive, to be quickly replaced by a secondary emotion, which can then complicate matters, as the secondary emotion may come from a more complex chain of thinking, so it becomes difficult to really know what is going on as in the case of anger arriving out of fear.

***

Here you will learn how to program yourself to experience more of the resourceful emotions you want in all the situations you want. The pictures you make in your imagination and the way you talk to yourself are all known as internal representations. And that is all they are, representations, not real life, so they cannot harm you.

Changes in breathing, muscle tension, posture, even facial expression, all influence your feelings and behavior, as you now appreciate.

Think of a time when you felt nervous, anxious, deflated. Notice how it affects your posture. Your shoulders slump and your head may have dropped.

I can show you a simple way to change. Wherever you are, plant your feet firmly on the ground, hold yourself tall, pull your shoulders back, take a great big breath in, let it out slowly, look up at the ceiling or the sky and put a great big grin on your face. Smile with your whole face with feeling. Now try to remember that tense situation again. Notice your mood has probably lifted and you no longer remember it in the same unpleasant way.

When you smile you exercise plenty of facial muscles. You're a bodybuilder, you should be exercising every muscle group including your face. Go on, smile.

Why not keep the feeling there. Stand straight, let your spine support you while you imagine a bright golden thread running up your spine and straight out to the sky. Let yourself relax, held up by the golden thread.

If your body is tense, it is producing different chemicals to when it was relaxed. Your heart rate may increase, or your blood pressure, so you feel and think differently. Notice how making physiological changes makes a difference to your emotional response.

And there's a lot said about pressure...

PRESSURE

"When you have fun,
it changes all the pressure into pleasure."
Ken Griffeyn

Pressure gets a bad name. It's the ultimate lie detector. When it's present it can be a positive force bringing out the best in you, or a negative one, being an excuse to quit. Some bodybuilders will break through, while those less committed break down. Everyone feels pressure, especially in competition, no one is immune. It can often start before the competition begins. Bodybuilders under pressure become internally self-conscious. Worrying about a posing mistake will probably get you one.

Recall a time when you felt pressure. Remember what you were doing, feeling, saying. Where you excited or nervous? Did you expect to lose or have a desire to win?

Did you allow all kinds of negative thoughts come into your mind?

Excessive mental pressure often produces mental blocks. Then anything recently learned in training may well be forgotten. Become mentally tough. Look at pressure as a challenge to drive yourself that much harder.

Pressure creates muscle tension, causing over-tightness, generally in the neck and shoulders. Heart beat goes up, breathing quickens, skin perspires. Some feel their stomach churn. These are all early physical warning signs. Mentally your mind starts racing. Negative, distracting thoughts come into your mind. When you are tense, you want to get your task over as soon as possible. The more you hurry, the worse you will be, creating even more pressure and greater muscle tension, so wasting more energy.

Did you know there is a relationship between mood and food? Foods high in refined sugars such as fizzy drinks, chocolate bars or biscuits, can increase blood sugar levels very quickly, giving a false high. When those effects dissolve, you quickly feel down, fatigued, with poor coordination due to your muscle groups using up the refined sugars too quickly. What you need is food which gives a slower, more natural release and assists your mood, like bananas and raisins to avoid the physical feelings of pressure.

Poise under pressure will be admired by many. They wonder how you do it. It is useful to recognize and become familiar with your own unique mixture of emotional reactions and physical reactions that appear during stressful times. Increased heart rate, muscle tension, loss of appetite, sweaty palms, impatience, irritability. How do you cope?

One effective method is simply to write down specific stressors. The simple act of recording a behavior you wish to change leads to improvements in the required direction.

For some people, a way to relax tense muscles is first tighten them further. If your shoulders feel like coiled springs, slowly draw them up and squeeze them. Hold for fifteen seconds. Feel the sensation. Then slowly release and relax completely. Notice how your shoulders feel.

Use travel time to listen to inspirational audio tapes or CD's. Hearing a person you admire and respect can have a positive impact on your mood. Upbeat music can make the miles fly by, or maybe something soothing to keep you calm en-route.

Stop reading this chapter right now and do the following breathing exercise. Close your eyes and take a deep breath down into your abdomen. Count slowly to three as you inhale through your nose and count to five as you exhale through your mouth. Do that five times.

You can enhance that deep breathing technique by remembering a time when you were having a great workout. As you breath and focus on that memory, say to yourself a word or phrase that can represent the relaxed feeling. Psychological research has shown deep breathing while reciting a simple word or phrase weakens even severe stress to some extent.

Days before an important event, a little nervousness may creep in. So the event actually starts before it starts. At home, the journey to the venue, in the changing room. How do you reduce pressure and place your mind in the hear and now? Here's one method to give yourself an advantage:

When you arrive in the changing room, use each article of clothing you remove, jacket, shirt, trousers, footwear, to let go of a concern or irrational fear. Each article of training kit you put on, imagine you're putting on resources of relaxation, courage or resilience. By the time you have changed, any distraction you had on your mind will have dissolved. Now you're in the right time zone and in the best state of mind for what's ahead.

Let's see how you can drive away the specter of anger...

ANGER & PSYCHING

"Learn to control your emotions or they will control you."

Edgar Martinez

Anger is born out of frustration and expectation. It feeds on itself. When you allow anger to get the best of you, it generally brings out the worst in you. As emotions go up, your capacity to behave in a calm, reasoned manner goes down. Anger blocks concentration. You may even get to despise yourself for losing it.

If you allow people or situations to tie you up in knots, your heart will beat faster and your breathing quickens. You're then stood there, all clenched jaw, staring eyes, tight muscles and hunched up shoulders, hacked off and out of control. Or you an learn from it.

You control your moods and emotions. If someone makes you angry, you are giving that person power over you. They are then controlling your moods and emotions. Anger can sometimes be fear in disguise, as anger is based on insecurity. Fighting spirit however is based on self-confidence.

Bodybuilders who cannot control themselves will never make great bodybuilders. The best have the maturity to master their emotions, not to be servants to them. That emotional energy allows you to raise yourself. Anger kept under control will work for you.

***

You cannot have a blind rage of anger if you remain calm. If you have an anger button, there is something you can do about it. While you're reading this chapter, get yourself relaxed as we are going to set a calm button as a resource before another anger moment arises. For convenience, we will set the anchors to your waist so you could do this standing at a treadmill or a weight machine and as you will look inconspicuous, nobody will have a clue what you are doing. However, you can set the anchors anywhere on your body that is appropriate. I will discuss *Anchors* more fully in another chapter.

Close your eyes and think of a recent time when you lost your cool, or think about the things that may trigger anger for you on a regular basis. Now, just for a few moments, really get back into it get fully immersed into that experience, see everything you saw to make you angry, hear everything you heard, feel exactly the way you felt.

Now step out of the experience as if you are watching someone else and rewind the scene as if you were rewinding a DVD until you reach the very first moment your anger began to develop. Go back a couple more frames and imagine there is a large red button and anchor that somewhere on your body, let's say on your left waist.

Now open your eyes and say your name backwards to break state then close your eyes again.

Now take three deep breaths, exhaling out longer than the in breath. Think of a relaxing time, a good holiday, being on a beach, a walk beside a lake, or a funny moment, something that makes you smile on the outside and on the inside. Really relax and get into the moment. Where do you feel that feeling? Let it spread throughout your body, going to the top of your head to the tips of your toes. See it as a color, feel it as a wonderful feeling or hear it as a sound.

As it begins to peak, imagine a big green button at your right waist, press this several times and let the feeling amplify.

Open your eyes. Say your name backward. Now press your red button and immediately after, push your green button and hold them both for a moment before releasing your red button while continuing to hold the green.

Repeat the sequence another half dozen times until triggering your green button automatically creates a calm response.

***

Psyching and gamesmanship are designed to upset you emotionally and disrupt your concentration. Recognize it for what it is and don't allow it to get inside your head and ruin your composure. If it affects you, it's there at the back of your mind. Even if you pretend it doesn't bother you, it does.

Also be aware there are two types of psyching – one someone else does and the one you do to yourself.

Come closer my friend. A way to divert anger is to divert your attention. Develop a ritual when you need to calm yourself or when you need a few moments to get yourself together. Pick a spot or a mark in the gym. Between sets, walk over to the mark and touch it, or if that is not possible, look at it. This can keep your mind focused while you give yourself a pep talk.

Or do something physical to slow events down for yourself. Rub your hands together, tighten your laces, rub a bar bell. Nothing too complicated. These are all small psychological boosts for mental and emotional management. When you can, change into dry kit, fresh socks, put on a sweat band, then take it off. Do some small change to make things feel like it's a new state.

You can always do unto others as they do to you and be as confrontational. Often they cannot take it. You are now taking the initiative. However, do you really need to lower yourself to their level? The best response is to be mature and have compassion for someone who has to resort to gamesmanship in trying to get one over you. Oh, and humor is a great weapon.

Let's calm ourselves with breathing...

BREATHING

Often overlooked, correct breathing should be carried out at all times, not only when you feel tense, as it calms your body and mind. When you breath normally, your body is subconsciously maintaining the balance of oxygen and carbon dioxide. When you are apprehensive, breathing changes to fast and shallow. This causes dizziness, poor vision, tiredness, breathlessness, which only increases further anxiety.

If you practice correct breathing, it becomes second nature. You must breath properly when you are anxious in any way as it will help keep you grounded.

High, or clavicular breathers only breath into the upper portion of their chests and lungs, so only a small amount of air can enter. Stale air remains in the lower lungs and impurities are not expelled. These people always seem to be gulping or gasping for breath and run out of air when they speak.

Most people use mid, or intercostal breathing but it is still not efficient as the chest is only partially expanded.

Low, deep, or abdominal breathing is the best effective way to take in reasonable amounts of air and to expel impurities from your lungs.

Where do you breath?

Lie on your back. Place one hand on your chest and the other on your abdomen. Breath all the way out to empty your lungs. Now, inhale in your normal fashion. Don't force it as you may get light-headed, in which case give it a rest till you feel better.

Which hand rises and fall the most? If it's the one on your chest, you're not breathing deeply enough. You should be breathing into your abdomen.

Here's how. Breath in through your nose and out through your mouth. Imagine a position an inch or two below your naval and you are sending each breath you inhale down to it. You should feel your stomach area swell as you inhale. If it does not, place something light, like a paperback book on your abdomen and as you inhale, concentrate on making the book rise. Watch a baby breath. Notice all the breathing action is at the abdomen. The baby has not been taught how to breath, the child is breathing naturally.

When you breath into your chest, you are only filling your lungs about three-quarters, the bottom quarter being stale air. Breathing into your abdomen actually fills the bottom of your lungs with fresh, rich air which can only do you good. While you breath into your abdomen and feel it expand, pull back your shoulders, drop your head back, then breath in some more to really fill your lungs from top to bottom. Very deep breaths are needed between sets to help you get through High Intensity Training.

Oxygen is energy. It helps relax the muscles and gives clarity to your mind. When you hold your breath, you create pressure and a nervous feeling develops. Slow, deep breathing will make you feel relaxed, improve the quality of your blood, generate good health, keeping your mind in the present.

When you look at the mechanics of breathing, you realize that inhaling or holding your breath the moment you carry out an exertion instead of exhaling is completely wrong. It places your body under strain as your energy is kept in rather than being released. Naturally exhaling at the point of exertion allows for more power and you feel your muscles working.

Here's a tip for training your abs. Air in the lungs prevents a full abdominal contraction, so always exhale before the contraction.

Slow, deep breathing will make you feel relaxed. Feeling more comfortable your ready to experience something new about relaxation...

RELAXATION

Some people might think of relaxation as sitting in front of the TV, going to the pub, spending time with family and friends. These may be relaxing times, but they still require a degree of emotional, mental and physical stimulation. True relaxation is a moment of emotional, mental and physical quiet. Your breathing and heart rate slows, your muscles relax and you feel calm and at peace in your body.

Here I will describe *progressive relaxation* which is basically a relaxation routine where you relax your muscle groups from the top of your head, all the way down to your toes. It was devised by Doctor Edmund Jacobson sometime in the 1920s as a simple way for a person to consciously relax whole muscle groups at a time and their mind. It is similar to the standard hypnotic induction and a way someone can consciously relax. It is an effective, but slow process.

Other therapists, mainly Richard Suinn, then Herbert Benson both in the 1970s modified progressive relaxation to speed it up. Now progressive relaxation is a proven, simple way of relaxing the muscles of your body and your mind.

Relaxation itself is valuable to health as it relieves mental and physical tension. When both your body and mind are at ease, other mental skills become unlocked, then your progress toward mental training, self=esteem, goal-setting and concentration will be smoothly accomplished.

Close your eyes if you want.

Take a deep breath and clench a fist tightly. Hold for three seconds, imagining the tension in the fist as a color, light or electricity, something that will represent tension for you.

Relax your fist as you exhale slowly. Imagine the muscle tension change color, light blue or green work well, or change the substance, feel it dissolving or melting away. Notice the difference in your hand before and after it was clenched and the relaxation it should feel now.

Do the same with your other hand, and in the future, you can clench both hands at the same time.

Breath in slowly, carry on with the muscles of both arms, really tense them, imagine the color or shape however you imagine the tension to be. Then release and exhale letting the color or shape to change. Let the arms relax and enjoy the feeling.

What other part of your body do you think we will relax next?

Onto your face. Really scrunch your face up and notice how good it feels when you relax it.

Shrug your shoulders, hold, then go through the relaxation procedure. Just let go!

Next your chest and back. Start to feel like a rag doll.

Now onto your waist.

Proceed to your hips and buttocks, breath in, tense and relax them.

As you breath out, you might think about the feelings in your legs. Tense your thighs, let them go. Feel yourself sinking into the floor.

Calf muscles now, getting soft and loose.

Finally your feet. Feel all the tension draining away.

Isn't it interesting how your body relaxes without trying too hard. Enjoy the feeling of calm. You can go through the progressive relaxation exercise as many times as you wish, just notice how relaxed you feel.

You can also do the exercise quickly. Tense and relax your upper body as a whole unit, then your lower body, then your legs. Relax that way in between sets.

You can utilize this relaxed state by making positive suggestions to yourself.

Another way to do this is without tensing your muscles, perhaps just before you sleep as you are lying in bed, as the movement of physically tensing your muscles may keep you awake.

Imagine a wave of relaxation soothing it's way down through your body, maybe it's a soft color, one that can really relax you, going into every fiber of your body. Remember a time of quiet and peace, a sanctuary perhaps or gazing at the stars on a clear summer evening or lying on a beach hearing the waves gently lap on the sea shore. Engage in the moment.

Here's an ideal method for instant physical relaxation which comes from yoga. Breath through your eyes. That's right! Imagine as you inhale, the air your breathing is entering your body through your eyes. You can actually feel your eye muscles relax whether your eyes are open or closed. It happens all by itself!

Now you know how to relax and use your imagination, let's see how you ask questions...

CREATIVE QUESTIONS

Asking questions is about the easiest and one of the most powerful tools you can use to transform yourself for the better and challenge your mind. Questions direct your focus of attention. If you do something poorly,simply ask yourself "how can I do this in a positive way?" which makes your questions more empowering.

Many sportspeople get frustrated because they ask themselves negative questions, beginning with "why can't I...?" To understand the question, your mind automatically looks for the reason why you cannot. But no matter what the answer is, you are still accepting the fact that you cannot do it. You are also reinforcing the problem in your mind. Here's a trick. Change 'why' into 'how.' Ask yourself, "how can I do...?" This assumes it can be done and there can be a number of ways it can be done, so the question allows your mind to search out a positive solution.

You will be surprised to discover how you can go further. You might ask, "how should I train my shoulders this week?" Instead ask "how should I train my shoulders this week to enjoy every minute?"

So, ask questions that focus on the positive:
How can this stamina problem be solved easily?
How can my protein consumption be improved?
How can I gain more muscle on my thighs?
How am I going to become...?

These questions put your mind into a more resourceful state. If you are not happy with an answer, change the way you ask the question. Your mind will keep searching until a happy solution is found. It's good to know your subconscious has the answers to all the questions you will ever ask. You can allow new answers to come to you, can you not?

Ask yourself these questions:
Do you love bodybuilding so much you would pay to do it?
What difference would it make if you could improve 10 – 20%.
What, if anything, is holding you back?

How passionate do you feel about bodybuilding?
What would you do if you had unlimited ability?

Curiosity creates questions. By bringing your vivid imagination into play as you ask creative questions, you build up a vivid representation of the answer, then amplify it. Make it a sensory-rich experience, turn the colors brighter, the sound louder, the feelings stronger. By regularly concentrating on what you want, you condition your mind to attract more of it.

***

If you find it difficult to bring an answer to mind, remember the solution to it! Remembrance was a Buddhist philosophers trick. Instead of asking your mind to search for an answer to a challenge, ask your mind to simply remember it. The presupposition that you once knew the answer creates a mindset that the answer actually exists, so eliminates the anxiety of helplessness.

Many apprehensions and worries are caused by not giving your mind something better to do. Look at it this way, the one asking the questions is usually the one holding the cards.

You may find decision making even more interesting with this method developed by Yvonne Oswald. How do you feel when you cannot make up your mind about a choice you have to make? It can become frustrating, I know. Begin to apply this strategy to small, daily decisions and build up to more important ones. Your subconscious understands your needs (not your wants) much better than you do consciously.

How you ask a question is important for clear decision making, so ask it like this, "how good is it for me to…?" which is far better to ask than, "do I want to…?" When you have a decision to make, ask the question that gives you a number between 0 and 10. Such as "how good is it for me to have a weight gain bar for breakfast?" The more quickly you can come up with an answer, the more you can place trust on your intuition. If the answer that emerges from any question is five or less, take the answer as a NO.

Ask yourself this, "how good is my gym for me right now?" If your answer is five or below, start looking elsewhere.

Other ways to ask questions are "is it best I increase the sets for my thighs to four?" or "will it be better for me to perform shoulder press with a machine or free weights?"

Test first to find out how much your subconscious mind is in touch by asking a true or false question, such as "my name is Bill," and notice what number between 0 and 10 reveals itself.

Good answers from good questions often come to you through rest…

REST

When we do bodybuilding, especially heavy weight lifting, there is often some micro damage caused to our muscle tissue because the will to fight and the will to win and make gains, makes our bodies tense and then injury may occur.

Both your mind and body have their own natural way to rest and recharge their batteries. This happens about every ninety minutes when they stop external focus and spend around fifteen minutes to rest and replenish. This is known as the *ultradian rhythm* when you find yourself daydreaming and a soft feeling of comfort begins in your body. People constantly ignore these signs so go into overload. If you go with it, you will feel refreshed and have better concentration after.

Deepen the experience by self-hypnosis, meditation, or listening to relaxing music. Imagine a favorite place, an exotic beach, an oasis of peace and calm, a garden, somewhere that is special for you. Your nervous system cannot tell the difference between a real or imagined event, so fool it into believing it's on holiday.

Do this exercise to improve well-being once or twice a day, it doesn't take long and it is a variation of the relaxation exercise I described earlier.

Put your attention on your feet and notice any feeling in them, coldness, warmth, weight.

Take a slow, deep abdominal breath and as you exhale, imagine a warm, pleasant feeling begin in your feet. You can imagine a color.

When you're ready, take another deep breath and imagine that warm, relaxed feeling traveling up to your knees. As it does, say a word like "rest" or "relax" or "peace" or give each stage a number. Let that comfortable feeling penetrate your muscles and bones, soothing them.

When ready, take another gentle breath and imagine the feeling rising up to your waist and repeat your special word, or the next number.

Do again up into your chest. .

With the same breathing pattern, let that feeling of ease and relaxation arrive at your shoulders, soothing them as you say your special word.

Next, let that relaxation flow from your shoulders down your arms and into your hands and fingers.

Again, breath and let the feelings flow all the way up your face to the top of your head. Say the word or number and let the feeling spread all over your body.

In your mind, say the word and imagine the relaxation double and float down from your head so it mixes with those good feelings already going on inside your body.

As this relaxation drifts down your body, imagine any tension being washed down and away out of your feet so it makes room for new, refreshing energy spreading down from your head, until you feel your body glow with energy from your head to your feet.

Now take a few moments to really bask in that feeling of relaxation.

If you want, do it again. The more you practice the better it becomes.

Just allow whatever happens to happen and feel satisfied with what you're accomplishing.

Maybe you will think about goals...

GOALS

"People are not lazy. They simply have impotent goals – that is, goals that do not inspire them."
Anthony Robbins

Can't get enough now, can you! A goal here is a mental representation of something you wish to achieve within a given time frame. Aiming for goals is a simple way to keep yourself motivated, evaluate progress, create emotion and achieve things. A goal can give you clearer direction. If you don't know where you are going, you will probably end up someplace else. Talent will take you just so far. Setting goals goes with mental training and hard work.

People don't deliberately plan to fail, but they fail to plan. What would you do if you knew you could not fail? Goals can stop you from stumbling through life. Why leave things to chance? Goals can help you move away from your limitations.

Setting goals is an art. Focus your mind on a target and you are more likely to hit it. If you don't aim for goals, all your efforts will go astray. And focus on what you want rather than what you don't want.

A well known acronym for setting goals is SMART. The S is for Specific. The more specific you make your goal, the easier it will become to figure out if you are on target and when you have achieved it. Bring in your senses when you form your goal so you can see, hear, feel everything as you visualize yourself achieving your desired outcome. Be careful about specific. "I want to gain four pounds of pure muscle this year." Is that specific? What happens when you reach your four pounds of pure muscle within eight months? "I want to gain more than four pounds of pure muscle this year," gives you room to go further.

M is Measurable. Create a starting point from where you can measure your improvements.

A stands for Achievable. High enough to inspire solid hope of reaching the goal. Only you know if your goal is achievable. Is it too challenging, or not challenging enough?

R is Realistic. Do you have the personal resources and skills to bring about your goal? Would more education be required? If the target is too big, too outlandish, far away, it can damage your motivation.

And T is Time-bound, an accomplishment date. If you do not set some form of deadline, tomorrow never comes. Keep it flexible, as reaching the goal is the important element, not the time frame. Set time limits, but keep them flexible, just reassess your goal and keep on until it is reached. Make goals challenging.

Hesitation ruins action. Stop putting things off, as with action you can aim for bigger, juicier goals. What do you want to accomplish in bodybuilding? It starts when you set goals. Setting goals is the first step into putting your dreams into action.

Ask goal-oriented questions:
What do you want from bodybuilding?
Is it specific, definite, measurable?
Can you maintain your goal?
What stops you having that goal?
What resources have you? Are they emotional, financial, mental, physical, spiritual?
What resources are required?

On a scale of 0 – 10, what would 10 be like as your very best? What would 3 be like? What is the closest to 10 you have been? Where are you on that scale now? What would it take to go 2 points higher? I bet you can do twice as good as you are doing.

How you design your goals makes a big difference. The bigger the better. Your goals should excite and scare you at the same time. If it frightens you, you are facing your fears of failure but your not backing down. Set your goals in concrete. "I'll do my best," or "let's see how it goes," does not carry much enthusiasm.

Break the ultimate goal down into smaller parts until each step is easy for you to take action. By having a number of smaller chunks to work on stops you from freaking out over a large, overwhelming one. State your goals with happiness and act as if they were already a reality. Read or recite your goal every day. Your mind needs constant repetition to accept your aims deeply and unconsciously. Be consistent.

Use your language carefully while designing goals. "I want to lose ten pounds of unwanted weight." Two words there confuse your subconscious, lose and weight. Why would you want to lose anything? Why do you want to weight (wait) to lose something? How about "I want to release ten pounds of fat in the next twelve weeks," makes it more direct. Get the point? You can then go to work with a new plan.

When you set your sights on a goal totally, your subconscious will do what it can to help you reach it. It does not take much to get things started, a simple thought or action. Or better, a thought and action combined.

Effective goals do several things. Higher goals lead to higher expectation. Conventional wisdom is right in suggesting we generally get what we expect. So if you set a modest goal, do not expect a higher-level result.

One of the reasons people do not reach a desired goal is they do not have a goal beyond it. Your goal becomes more motivational when other possibilities are likely once you have achieved it.

However you are getting on, rejoice when you reach about three quarters (75%) of your goal to celebrate how far you have come and remain upbeat.

Goals give you growth. They can transform your life. Take notice of anything at all that shows you are achieving your target or what motivates you toward that target. Hold it in your hands, smell it, let it shine on you.

I cover more on goals in the *Self-Hypnosis for Bodybuilding* Appendix which comes later.

Let's change any negative self-talk by re framing...

RE FRAMING

> *"Little things affect little minds."*
> Benjamin Disraeli

Don't mistake a temporary set-back as failure. Failure is not the end result. Some see failure as an excuse to give up, others think about failure so much, it becomes the best way to attract it. Others, you included, can see things in a positive light by re framing any situation. The glass becomes half full, never half empty. As you are in control, re framing gives you the flexibility to make situations work for you.

In training, do you ever think you may never transform your body to how you want it? Do you worry you may lose your next competition. Or is that why you have never entered one? Thoughts like these hamper you. If your afraid about losing, your dominant thought is about losing. Winners think about the next competition and how to prepare for it, losers think about the last one and who to blame. Notice your thoughts and make them positive.

There is a principle in physics known as the *Heisenberg Uncertainty principle*. This teaches us when you change the way you look at something, that something changes in response. Look differently at your challenges and redirect the power of your mind to succeed in bodybuilding.

When you come across a competitor who seems bigger or more experienced than you, do not tell yourself s/he is better than you and defeat yourself. Use your internal dialogue to play on any weakness they have, real or imagined. In your mind change their appearance, remember how to do that in the *Imagination* chapter? This gives your mind something to do and gives you the confidence to challenge them. Being more relaxed, you can focus more easily on your posing and stop any negative self-talk which could cause tension.

Positive thinking helps you realize there are limitations in any opponents ability, as discussed in the *Imagination* chapter. Look for their weaknesses, not strengths and create emotion when you speak to yourself. Be delighted with yourself, your opponent is after all, only human.

Know that if you have damaging thoughts, you can change or remove them. To make any negative emotion disappear, amend the thought. Imagine it as a form, change any color, put a frame around it, make it smaller, further away, make it darker. Move the sound, change it. When you have changed the negative emotion, repeat the routine several more times so it can't affect you again.

***

Another re frame can be done if you don't usually get pictures or sounds, but experience negative feelings. This is similar to the voice moving exercise in *The Inner Critic* chapter:

Where is the feeling? Move it to your thumb or big toe.
Does it have a shape? Change the shape.
What texture does it have? Change that.
What temperature has it? Turn it cold or warm.
Change any element until all the negative feeling is eliminated.

Whenever you realize you make a negative statement, restate what you said into a positive one by beginning the sentence with "in the past." "I can't exclude carbs before a show," now becomes "in the past I could not exclude carbs before a show."

Re framing can transform you, bring hope from hopelessness, turn despair into delight, build success from apathy. As with everything taught here, you have to practice, then practice some more, but once you know it, you have it for life.

New thinking = Better thinking = Better ability = Better you.

We often brand ourselves failures when we forget our successes. Look at any setback as time for change. Go for the change, don't be afraid.

Re framing can be helped by anchoring...

ANCHORING

"Don't find fault, find a remedy."

Henry Ford

Remember how you can use *The Circle of Excellence* to bring about a resourceful state? So with anchoring. It's like having a push button to feel excellence.

Anchors exist all around you. Have you ever come across an old photo which created a pang of nostalgia. Heard an old song which was popular during a special time in your life? Smelt a particular aroma that brought memories rushing back? Do you frequently visit a location and always sit in the same place, or go to the gym and work at the same stations in the same sequence?

All these associations trigger memories that take us back to a past experience. They are called 'anchors' as they anchor you to a certain emotional state. The clever thing is you can use these anchors to bring back a whole good experience.

The theory behind using what is known as a 'resource anchor' is if you constantly link the mood or emotion you desire to be in, with a meaningful feeling, picture, sound, or even taste or smell, you can reproduce that desired mood or emotion when you need it.

The process to set up a resource anchor only takes a few minutes. Read the routine a couple of times to get it clear in your head. Now think of the resourceful state you would like to have. Only choose one resourceful state at a time:

Create for yourself a physical signal which you are going to use. What you read in many NLP books is to touch your thumb and forefinger together, but it can be anything which you think is appropriate, like patting down your hair, scratching an imaginary itch on your cheek, clasping your hands, rubbing a knee, crossing fingers, it is up to you. Those are examples of physical triggers, however saying a certain word , phrase or mantra may do the trick for you.

Now, think vividly of a time when you had the ability or emotion you want to repeat. Rewind the clock, add as much detail as you can. Remember what you saw, hear what you heard, feel how you felt then. Now see, hear and feel all that even more fully. Experience it again intensely.

Let it all come back to you, let it build up so you relive it in your whole body. If you cannot remember a time, imagine how you would feel if you had that confidence, success or joy.

As the good memory returns and begins to build up to a peak, fire the physical signal or whatever trigger you have set. Sink into that feeling of being there again. Make it brighter, richer, turn up the volume. The peak, when you are in the right state, generally lasts between five and fifteen seconds on average, but for some individuals it could be two seconds, while for others almost a minute.

Now think about an unrelated topic, something like remembering a friends telephone number, saying your name backwards, or reciting the first few bars of a nursery rhyme, so when you repeat the technique, it's like doing it afresh.

Now repeat the technique four or five times, breaking state between each.

When you decide the resource anchor is functional, break state for the last time. Test to see if the anchor works. Break state by thinking of something else, then fire the anchor. You should now get back into the resourceful state. If not, apply the stimulus several times more and test again.

There is usually a couple of things going on if you are having trouble. Make sure you are actually re-living the whole event rather than just thinking about it. You must fel the positive emotion, after all, emotions are energy in action. Have one specific resource or event in mind rather than getting confused juggling several. Do you understand the process fully? If not, go over it again.

It gets better. Whenever you are experiencing that resource in your normal life, anchor it with the same stimulus you devised so you are topping up.

Thee great thing about using anchors is they work automatically. Think about a forthcoming event when you will require a particular feeling or emotion. Imagine everything going perfectly. Picture in your mind, seeing, hearing, feeling yourself in this good state at the future time. Now fire your anchor.

Do it when you are in different environments. Go to different locations and practice getting yourself into positive moods. You can look back with satisfaction to see how much further you have developed.

You can create resourceful states for those you train. If working with someone, it's ideal for you to be in the same resourceful state as they want to be in. If any states, or emotions your student wants, appear to contradict, like being motivated but relaxed, ask your student if they feel they can be in both states at the same time. If they believe they can, all well and good. If not, it's best to create two different anchors, one for motivation and another for relaxation which you apply separately.

***

You see how you can become anchored to certain states. Unfortunately you may even have created unresourceful states for yourself in the past. We all have negative anchors which can be disconnected by a process called 'collapsing anchors.'

Ensure you understand the method fully and you feel comfortable with it. Unless you're a trainer applying this with one of your students, it's best to have someone go through this process with you as you may need help to fix the anchors in place.

Agree fully what the negative state is to be collapsed and decide what resourceful state is going to replace it. Make sure you are replacing a negative state with a very strong, positive one:

Decide where on your body you are going to apply the resource and remove the negative state from. To keep things simple, you would apply the resourceful stimuli to one side of your body, be it the right knuckle, or right elbow, or right knee, then remove the negative state from the opposite left knuckle, left elbow, left knee.

On a scale of 0 – 10, how do you/the student feel about the situation? Remember, if working with a student, have them fully relive the event intensely and as the good feeling peaks, they should give you a prearranged signal, a nod of the head for example so you can then anchor the resource in position.

Access fully a positive state or memory you or your student have experienced, let's say competence and anchor that to say the right knee. Do this several times then test to check if the anchor works.

Break state by thinking of something else. This is important.

Now, once only, fully remember the unwanted state or memory, for example we'll say apprehensive. Relive it and when you/they feel the emotion peak, anchor it onto the opposite side of the body, in this case, the left knee.

Break state then test that anchor works.

Here's the good part. Fire both anchors simultaneously. Continue holding the positive anchor (right knee) for about five seconds while releasing the negative anchor immediately (left knee). As long as the resourceful states anchor is stronger than the undesired states, the undesired anchor will collapse and the UN-resourceful state will now longer be effective. If you picked a strong, negative memory, you may need more resources to make the situation more satisfying.

Test by asking how you or your student feels about the issue on a scale of 0 – 10.

Future pace by imagining some time in the future when you/they would confront that issue again and notice the response. If the problem has gone, continue imagining the old problem at a number of future events weeks, months or even a year into the future until you are certain the problem has gone.

Next is a method to overcome internal conflict...

INTERNAL CONFLICT

Part of you may have the confidence to step up to High Intensity Training, while another part of you may want to be cautious, perhaps because of a past injury. A tug-of-war between ambition versus caution. Two conflicting beliefs you have for the same situation can only hold you back.

If two incompatible states occur at the same time, you can modify each and reform them into a third state, which is an integration of the original two.

Throughout this book, you will learn methods which will get your mind working. Some may seem silly, others uncomfortable. Some may challenge your way of thinking, but change does that. Take it as a good sign, it's not for the fainthearted.

This process can cause changes:

Taking the example of two conflicting beliefs as above, confidence and caution, find a quiet place where you are not going to be disturbed and get yourself relaxed. Think about the situation that is causing internal conflict.

Place your hands in front of yourself, palms up. Imagine a confident part in your dominant hand. See it as a color, shape, a person, anything to make it real for you.

Do the same with your other hand, where you place your cautious part.

Ask the confident hand what is it's positive intention is for you. Continue asking until you get the feeling of an answer at the subconscious level, even if you think you are imagining it.

Next, ask the cautious hand what it's positive intention is for you.

Keep asking until you recognize on some level, they both want the same outcome. Go through the process even if you think your imagination is playing tricks, it's not.

This is for reference:
Confident part = more courage = train harder = success.
Cautious part + anxious = safety = success.

Now imagine a successful part is there, between your hands, possessing the resources of confidence and caution.

Slowly bring your hands together until those two separate parts become an integrated whole.
Bring your joined hands up to your chest and imagine your allowing the new, integrated part to step inside you. Convinced?

You can do that when two opposing emotions develop from the same event. When you are calm but feeling aggressive, relaxed but tense, nervous but confident.

***

Next is a slightly different, quick method to change a negative response into a positive:

Bring to mind a problem or bad memory you have. What would it's solution or opposite be where you want a desirable outcome?
Place your non-dominant hand about eighteen inches in front of your face and project the problem onto it. Have your dominant hand behind your back.
Practice by changing hands so your dominant hand is before your face, the other behind your back. Now intend to project the solution onto your dominant hand.
Now you know the movement, get set up as before with the problem hand before your face and as fast as you

can, change hands. You can even use a motivational word as you change.

Break state by shaking your hands, repeat your telephone number or use some other distraction.

Repeat ten times. You should neutralize the problem and replace it with a beneficial condition.

As you practice it gets easier to resolve any internal conflict.

You can hold onto your seat as you are about to enter the world where there are no limitations. Let's talk about motivation...

MOTIVATION

"You just can't beat a person who never gives up."
Babe Ruth

Motivation is a much used word in sport. It comes from the Latin word meaning 'to move.' The most important thing for you however, is to love your bodybuilding.

Most people can access unhappiness, guilt, even depression quite easily. By thinking of some failure in your life you open up an undesirable emotion. Fortunately the opposite can be the same. You can feel confident, excited, happy. You don't have to have a reason!

If you have had a great cardio session, you can repeat it by accessing the same level of arousal that you experienced at that great session. Here are some methods to do that.

Change livens things up, you can vary your training routine, different exercises, new locations.

Decreasing your rate of breathing will affect your nervous system. Slow, deep breathing through your nose creates relaxation in your body and mind.

Someone could call nervous energy before a competition anxiety. You could label it excitement. Rename nervousness, boredom, drudgery to something more inspiring. How does another type of excitement sound, or adventurous.

Release any tense, nervous energy by moving the muscles. Tense and relax each muscle group. You should do this during a warm up anyway. Waiting to go onto the stage, you could shift from foot to foot to sway into a relaxed, calm state of awareness.

Use key words that can excite, or inspire you. 'Easy, now, power, winner,' even your name. Create words or phrases that are personal, but powerful for you.

Use upbeat music to arouse you.

Suppose you have an exercise you don't like. Picture something that motivates you, then trick yourself into changing it so it looks and feels exactly the same as one that gets you going. As you have learned, altering the variables, brightness, color, position, shape, sound, can change how you react.

These are the steps:

Remember something that pleased you, a triumph you would wish to experience again. Concentrate on that image while you ask yourself:
Is it a still picture or a movie?
Is it in color or black & white?
Is it close to you or further away?
What size?
Are you inside it, like it is wrapped around you, or outside and you are looking in?
If any movement, is it fast or slow?
If the image is in front of you, are you looking from above, or below it?
Look at the exercise you don't like. Ask yourself the same questions and notice what's different or the same about the two pictures.
Move the exercise picture into a space occupied by the triumphant picture. Change everything to make it look and feel the same as the triumphant picture.
Intensify it, make it vibrant. Give it more of what you have given it. Hear the band playing a theme tune! Even imagine gentle pressure on your back as if someone was pushing you into the scene.

Do the change quickly, forcefully, five times. Break the state between each change, so you're starting it new each time.

By telling your brain to represent the exercise picture in this exciting new way, the happy changes you make tell your brain "I don't want this, I want this!" So, how do you feel about that exercise now? It should feel better, more achievable.

Remember earlier, by changing 'why' into 'how' can be inspiring? Here's another word to change to get that motivation flowing. 'Should' gives people a feeling of guilt when they 'should do, but don't.' Turn it into 'want.' "I should work my calf muscles." How does that make you feel in your body? Let it become "I want to work my calf muscles." Is that 'want' feeling different from 'should?' Has it made you more determined? Does it give you a prideful desire to achieve? Want power can be as good as will power.

As I have mentioned, use language carefully. Words represent something, they are symbols. Your words can literally become your world. Here's some more you can play with:

Turn 'but' into 'and,' 'if' into 'when,' 'why' can also become 'because.' Here's some more. 'Hopefully or might' can be "I'm going to" or "I am capable." These words can be more motivating.

Change your training routine every four to six weeks. Do different exercises for the same muscles, extend your range. Have cardio sessions, fat burning sessions, exercise to failure sometimes. All these changes to your routine all help to avoid boredom, avoid over-training and create further challenges. It's always good to take a week off as this gives time for micro tears to recover and I have always found I have increased enthusiasm when returning to the first training session after a week's rest.

Finish these statements:
I'm in the process...
I've decided...
It excites me when...

Let's investigates the power of mirroring...

MIRRORING

*"A champion is afraid of losing,
everyone else is afraid of winning."*
Billie Jean King

Anything practiced continuously over time becomes an automatic behavior. Problems arise when the practice is not perfect. If it's not spot-on you create a wavy, varied pathway to the required standard.

Even as an adult, you can still find a place for role models who have the physique and represent and support the standards you embrace and you should never outgrow your appreciation for this type of person who can be an invaluable inspiration for you.

If you are new to bodybuilding, you have nothing to personally use as a reference to achieve a particular level. Copy the same things in the same way as someone who has excelled at it. Choose a role model, someone you respect, admire. Arnold, Frank Zane, someone who has walked that road. Get yourself a DVD if you are able. Watch out for the subtle information. Imagine what having their body can do for you.

Become a director and make a movie in your mind of your role model training or performing effortlessly. Press play and watch carefully as your hero does everything perfectly from beginning to end. Watch out for any distinctions you need to note.

Observe how your role model carries him/herself. How do they move? How do they talk to themselves positively? This time, play the movie again, including yourself beside or behind your role model, imitating their actions, breathing, voice, mimic everything exactly.

Now climb in and disguise yourself as your hero, synchronize fully. Modify everything until the animation is exactly as you wish. See through their eyes, hear through their ears, take on the feeling of how empowered s/he is.

Feel what it's like to be your role model. Having that body. Build up the feelings, sounds, sights. See all around you how other people respond.

How different does your future look? How much more optimism do you have as a result of owning this body? Live this future. Make it real for yourself.

Step out and away and imagine in front of you another you who now exhibits the assurance, energy and body you have made your own. Make any modifications.

If your role model has written a book or articles, has photos, get a copy to study. Do research. Find out what that person did to find success. Understand how they think.

Continue to rehearse until you are certain you can be like that role model. Even if you feel like yoe making it up, your teaching your brain new behavior, so pretend until it becomes natural.

***

It's a valid thought that mirroring can oversimplify the topic of achieving success as it does not take into consideration natural talent. An example would be your physical condition and attributes. Some people are genetically gifted, many are not. You may never have the potential to become a world champion. If you were to examine the world champions, you would find patterns in their diets, lifestyle, training and mindset. Duplicating these patterns is not a guarantee you will duplicate their professional level, but it will guarantee you will become as good a bodybuilder or figure competitor as you can be, given your genetic potential.

Also imagine sometimes other factors that may hinder you, so you can bring other emotions into it. Do not only imagine the best-case scenarios, be prepared with a Plan B and a Plan C. Don't imagine failing, but mentally plan how you will respond to unpleasant or difficult situations. They happen sooner or later when things don't go exactly as you hoped. You can still be proud of putting 100% effort in.

When mirroring or modelling a world great, you will never step into his or her footsteps I'm sorry to say. But what you will do is leave your own tracks. Anything is possible and they will be your own tracks. Pretend you're an exceptional bodybuilder, act as if it were true and soon your mind forgets to pretend.

Feeling good? Want to create happiness on demand? You can with the inner smile...

THE INNER SMILE

When you are happy your body creates a chemical, serotonin, known as the happy chemical. It releases tension, controls pain, gives your immune system a boost and promotes well-being throughout your body.

Remember times when you were happy and lighthearted. If you cannot think of a particular time, how about a comedy show or a film you have seen, even jokes you have heard. Go over them while you turn up the brightness, the color, the sounds, make them richer, remember how good you felt until you find yourself smiling with pure joy. Double that feeling. Do it again. How do you feel?

Imagine now how better your life can be if you were like this all the time. Happiness plays an important role in your success. Imagine when you have read this chapter how good and refreshed you will feel.

Vividly imagine your eyes smiling, a glint dancing in them. Raise the corners of your mouth as if you have a special secret. You use plenty of facial muscles when you smile so give them a good workout.

Get a sense of where that happy feeling is the strongest. Play with it some more. Increase it, give it a happy color and roll it up to the top of your head and down to the bottom of your feet. Imagine every cell glowing with delight. You can do this anywhere. It's good to imagine all the benefits this is going to give you, isn't it?

Put a smile anywhere in your body that feels uncomfortable or tense. When you think about relationships, training, diet, smile with the same energy and notice your mood begin to lift.

Here's a bonus. These happy chemicals create more connections in the brain every time you have a pleasant experience. So not only can your body experience happiness, the more intelligent you become. What was a technique has now become a positive attitude.

And the more positive you can be with relationships...

RELATIONSHIPS

P T Barnum

This chapter is on the basis of people you know involved in bodybuilding.

Often it can be family, friends, training partners who are a barrier to what you want to achieve. "You will never be good enough," or "don't set your sights to high." As well meaning as they think they are being, they make it easier for you to feel worse, not better. Have you ever noticed how expert some people can be about things they don't have a clue about. If you take notice of people who tell you what you cannot do, you will never accomplish anything. These negative people place you in a negative frame of mind, you have a conflict of priorities making you question you own abilities.

Then there are intolerant, or ill-informed trainers. They think they are being helpful by criticizing you. Some people do respond to that, but it doesn't work for everybody. Often you have a workout feeling demotivated because a negative expectation has been set up in your mind.

Don't take it seriously. Relaxation or humor is an antidote.

Have you had an argument with a training partner or the gym manager and hours later you are still re-living it? Still seeing their face and hearing their words. If you change the picture and sounds as described in the chapter on *Imagination*, you can change your feelings.

What about a conflict of ideas with your instructor. Perhaps you should consider what they have said before dismissing it. Rationalize first. The truth can hurt sometimes, but putting yourself in others shoes makes you adaptable, so giving you further insight.

Go to a time when you had a difference of opinion. Visualize that person stood before you now, notice all their details.
Now step out of your body and let any emotions go. This will soon start to make sense.

Step into their body and notice the world from their perspective, seeing, hearing, feeling and thinking from their point of view.

Next, step away from their body and let their feelings go.

Think of someone you admire, a friend, hero, Saint, a character from the past who is mature, intelligent and wise. Step into their body and be that person considering you and your foe from a neutral position. Are there any insights that come to mind? What advice would this mentor give you?

Lastly, step back into your own body, taking with you anything you have learned. Can you move toward a resolution? Do you see things differently?

***

A key to reaching your potential is learn to listen to others. Lean toward them when they speak. Place your tongue onto the roof of your mouth, this quietens internal dialogue so you can pay attention to the other person. Don't interrupt or finish their sentence. People will appreciate your listening skills. If someone interrupts while you are speaking, politely ask them to wait until you have finished then you will listen while they speak.

Follow your goals and not the crowd. You may feel envious when your friends go to parties, often the parties aren't that much anyway. You can make up for it later.

When outside influences and social pressures are removed, you are far more able to achieve your desires. Avoid people or distractions that can turn you away from your dreams. Sometimes you may have to let go of old friendships if a fire to succeed as a bodybuilder burns in you.

One of the best ways to improve is to mix with successful, skillful people. Surround yourself with achievers who provide good teaching and will make you better. Find a few bodybuilders, trainers, judges, journalists, anyone who understands the sport. Invite them out for a coffee or a meal. Be cheeky. Write to them for advice. Let them know you want to pick their brains on how you can become a success. They become aware of you and understand you are serious. Be humble. Listen. As long as you are respectful, most people will enjoy the opportunity to help you. Others can also see situations without the emotional baggage you may be carrying.

Take advantage of the experiences trainers and veteran bodybuilders have had. They have lived the challenges you face and how to deal with them, or where they have failed so you can learn from their mistakes. Ask a regional, national or international winner their keys to bodybuilding success. What have they done? How did they do it?

Praise others also. Being critical, judgmental or opinionated are just three ways to see relationships disappear. Use integrity. Impart sound knowledge and experience to others younger than you. Set an example.

Excitement and passion are contagious. Don't allow others to put you off or pull you down. And remember, scientists proved bumblebees could not fly. The scientists didn't tell the bumblebees! You have more potential than you or others realize.

Next, let's look at the interesting subject of time management...

TIME MANAGEMENT

"Put your hand on a hot stove for a minute, it seems like an hour. Sit with a pretty girl for an hour, it seems like a minute."

Albert Einstein

You cannot control time, it just moves on. If you are tired or don't feel like training, the clock still ticks away. You cannot buy time, save it, trade it or make it. Each and every moment passed is a moment gone that will never pass again. Your time therefore is valuable to you. The good thing about time is it's free.

If you cannot control time, you need to know how to manage what you do with your time. Remember your goals? Have you thought about them today? Remain focused on your goals as they will help you arrange your days.

Most of us find it difficult to live in the present, we think about past experiences and worry about future ones. Time passes at different rates for each of us. Your subconscious mind does not compare time passing the same way as your conscious mind, which does so by the clock, watch or other time piece.

Time varies depending on the circumstances you find yourself in. When you're nervous, in pain or sad, time slows down. The clock seems to drag, a couple of minutes are like half-an-hour, or even stands still. Long, boring periods warming up and waiting to go out to perform can cause you to lose concentration and sharpness.

In contrast, when you are excited and happy, maybe having a great workout with good friends, time flashes by.

You can manipulate time if you imagine a situation and slow the process right down to practice and improve a technique.

As I've said, the subconscious mind does not recognize fact from fiction, so this can be done to learn a new movement, stimulate muscle, or rehearse for a show and is an ideal method if you are resting an injury which is best not to be physically moved. This can help you stay focused. I'll show you:

Get into a relaxed state. If you are better closing your eyes, do so. You can hold a real dumbbell or lifting bar in your hands to make it more real, or pretend there is. Feel the weight, the coolness of the iron. Smell that fake tan or oil. Bring in every sense while you remain comfortable.

Carefully examine the correct movements of the exercise. Feel for yourself the whole process, go over each step in strict form, so you can physically remember the movements of grip and the full extension and contraction of the muscles being exercised.

See each element of the movement in slow motion. Go over them several times making sure each part of the technique is right. When you are happy, speed it all up. Imagine doing the exercise for real. Feel mighty, make everything colorful, vivid, breath as you would lifting for real, feel the muscles working.

With every mental rehearsal you do, the details will increase. The practice you can make in your mind in a few minutes, would require hours of practice in real time. Your subconscious cannot tell the difference between what is real and what is imagined, which is why this method is ideal if you are out through injury. It can help keep you focused.

Enjoy the activity as you see yourself perform at your best. And give yourself positive suggestions.

***

Here is an easy activity to help place bodybuilding as your number one daily priority. Get yourself a calendar, diary or a day planner. If it pictures bodybuilding, so much the better. Start your day with it by writing down the time you plan to train, compete, read a motivational book. Then plan the rest of your day around that event, no matter what. Make this a daily commitment. You have made bodybuilding your top priority and arranged everything else around it rather then trying to fit bodybuilding in.

In the next chapter you are going to learn to conquer fear...

FEAR

(False Evidence Appearing Real)

"It's not a question of getting rid of butterflies, it's a question of getting them to fly in formation."

John Donohue

We all have a primitive flight or fight response built into us for survival. This response will be explained more fully in the *Pain Control* chapter. We either freeze, faint, fight or flee from whatever is threatening us. Today, most of our dangers are not a threat to life or limb, but a psychological threat to our self-esteem and ego.

What I am going to discuss here is not a sport technique itself, however some bodybuilders do go through anxieties. You might be uneasy in lifts, afraid of cats, dogs or birds. You don't like flying and you are off to a foreign location. These can all make your stomach tremble, creating limitations for you which could turn into a phobia.

You were not born with a fear or phobia. Many phobias can be traced back to an unpleasant incident when you were younger. Your elder brother may have locked you in a cupboard when you were a child. What if the dark cupboard was full of moths, or even spiders! Since then, whenever you see moths, spiders or when you are in an enclosed space, you relive the event.

The fear of failure prevents many people from reaching their full potential. Fear actually creates the situation that stops bodybuilders from being winners. Fear creates a feeling of vulnerability. A paradox is that fear of failure actually makes failure more likely.

An injury can create a fear response as you may be scared of hurting yourself again then suffering the agony of more recovery time. It can be difficult getting your mind around a comeback after suffering a serious injury. There can be a lot of Adrenalin pumping around when you start training again.

Look at it this way. A fear, even a phobia, is an overcompensating protection mechanism. You did not learn it, you over-learned it and the good news is, because it was learned, it can be changed and unlearned.

The following technique is known as *The Fast Phobia Cure* or *The Movie Theater Cure.*

Close your eyes and get comfortable. Give this your full involvement. Imagine you are sat in a cinema, you can remember a real one if you wish. The screen is blank. You are in charge of a remote control there in your hand.

On a benchmark of 0 – 1-, with 0 being nothing at all, with 10 being extremely severe, what number would your problem be? How high is it?

In a moment you are going to play a movie of yourself and the problem you have. As it is a past event, the movie has aged, so it's poor quality and the color has faded, even turned sepia. You will play your movie in a rectangle in the center of the screen, not all of the screen.

Compose a comical theme tune, something like The Muppets, Monty Python, Popeye or similar.

Before you press play, remember a time when you knew you were confident, excited or successful. Feel all that good energy and let it spread all around your body, then intensify it. Turn up the volume. Maintain that good feeling while you watch the movie. You may even use anchoring to create a resourceful state if the fear your facing should get out of hand.

Now pay attention. Behind you is the cinema projection booth. To get an even further distance from your fear, imagine yourself leaving your body sat there in the chair and float up, back toward the projection booth. From here, you can observe yourself watching the movie through the projection window, watching yourself on the screen.

You will play the film of your bad event from the beginning to the end where it will then freeze-frame. Go ahead and press play on the remote.

When the film reaches that last frame, press stop. Now watch yourself in the cinema seat rise up and go up there to the still picture and congratulate the younger you for being so brave for going through and surviving that nasty experience. You're safe. With that acknowledgment, watch yourself return to your seat.

When your ready, run the whole film backward at top speed, hearing that comical music play. Then play the movie forwards, then backwards at fast speed several times. How do you feel? Is there a difference to the memory? Has the old response gone? Where is the problem now on the scale from 0 – 10? How low is it? If reduced slightly, you can go through the exercise again to reduce it further until that memory no longer bothers you. When you're ready, float back down to your seat and feeling fully whole again, rise and exit the cinema.

Feel the fear, feel the doubt. Know there will be uncertainty, then go ahead anyway. Champions interpret those signals as signs to move forward and become pro-active instead of reacting protectively. When you encounter fear, doubt, uncertainty, ask yourself is it a genuine danger? Can it really hurt you? Is it part of growth? We all get anxious, but people plagued by fear get anxious about being anxious. Accept fear and recognize it as the body telling you to become energized. You can face any difficulty and come out smiling.

Or try spinning...

SPINNING

This is a simple, quick-fix technique taught by Paul McKenna who I acknowledge here for it. You may find it interesting. It's ideal when you find yourself in a shaky or stressful situation which needs to be addressed there and then. The concept is all feelings start in one place within your body and move in a prescribed direction and so by reversing the direction of the bad feeling, you can eliminate it.

Go through this routine while thinking about your problem. On a scale of 0 – 10 with 0 being nothing and 10 being extremely uncomfortable, where are you at the moment thinking about your concern? How high is it?

Thinking about the disturbance, get an idea of where that feeling begin. Usually it starts around the stomach/solar plexus and moves upward toward your throat.

Imagine lifting that feeling out of your body and watching it spin before you like a wheel.

Imagine what color it is. Now change that color to a favorite.

Maybe imagine a pleasant noise or calm music.

With a flip, turn the wheel upside down so that it spins in the opposite direction.

When you feel calmer about the situation, pull the wheel back into your body to where it started, still spinning in the opposite direction.

Let it speed up, faster and faster, until the anxiety or upset begins to fade away and finally disappear.

On the scale of 0 – 10, where do you find that problem now? How low is it? Problems can vanish entirely.

You can also replace an undesirable state with a desirable one by using swish...

SWISH

This strategy can bring freedom to self-doubt. The trick is to have your positive image on the catapult in it's high tension position, ready to fire so that your mind accepts the image as going one way – toward you.

In front of you place a mega body picture of the image you would like of yourself. Something that can give you goose bumps of excitement. Assertive, powerful, or remember a memory you would like to change. Something that is realistic and attainable. Make the image exciting. Have the image full of the skills or qualities you would like more of. Make the details vivid, see yourself oozing confidence, then make it larger, the colors bright, add sparkle, play a theme tune that's up-beat, adding vitality. Add approving voices of trainers or judges. Make everything rich and intense. I really want you to live in this so include anything that improves the image.

Imagine this picture has thick rubber bands attached to each corner and are fixed at the other end to a firing mechanism next to you. The picture is slowly pulled away from you, stretching off into the distance on those rubber bands, so that it seems like a giant catapult is being aimed at you ready to fire. Lock that exciting picture in place and be aware of the tension in those stretched rubber bands. Your hands are on the firing lever.

Bring up a second image or memory before you of whatever it is that's giving you a lack of confidence, fear, inertia, where you would benefit from a new self-image. Drain away any color, turn down the focus, shrink it down, quieten any sound. Go on, play with it.

You are about to fire that first, good image but before you do so, think of an inspirational word to use as you fire. Originally it was "swish" as that is how therapists had the two images interchanged, but any word appropriate to you or the situation can be more effective.

When you are ready, fire the catapult so that the exciting image shoots up right in front of you, it's acceleration tearing through that poor second image or memory, so you end up with that exciting picture before you. If it's done fast enough, you may even jump. Don't forget to add the inspiring word.

Notice any changes to how you feel. Reset the positive image by stretching back the elastic band again under tension so you have before you the remnants of the broken second image, of what had made you feel bad. With that poor picture in front of you, fire again so that the good picture once more rips through the bad, blasting through it once more.

Do this five times. Each time that positive image shoots toward you, it ends bigger and brighter and the poor image is reduced until the last time, when it is completely destroyed.

Another technique to reduce or eliminate problems is through tapping...

TAPPING

"Human feelings are words expressed in human flesh."

Aristotle

Meridian energy systems have been demonstrated by Paul McKenna on TV. They are safe, fast and easy to do. The cause of all negative emotions is a disruption in the bodies energy system. You have a negative thought and then you have a negative response which creates noise in your energy system. By using meridian energy systems you can collapse that emotional disruption.

Originally created by Dr Roger Callahan, a psychologist trained in acupuncture and applied kinesiology. He devised TFT (Thought Field Therapy) by insights from those fields as a psychological version of acupuncture. TFT uses a lot of points, used in a specific order in a certain sequence.

Gary Craig, a master practitioner of NLP took TFT and distilled it into a simpler version known as EFT (Emotional Freedom Technique) which has become much more widely used and is more accessible for anyone to learn as they tap in a prescribed sequence while distracting your mind to reduce the unpleasant experience.

Other systems have followed on from EFT. TAT, BSFF, Emo trance. They all deal with healing any imbalance in the energy system and some have modified EFT.

This procedure seems to access the meridian energy system where any emotions become trapped. The tapping creates vibrations in the energy system which appears to release the original energy disturbance and restores the even flow, somewhat like tapping on your central heating pipes to clear an air lock.

Unconvinced? Like any of the techniques in this book, it seems strange at first, but it is based on scientific fact and has produced quick, substantial changes for many.

For convenience, I will describe the version demonstrated by Paul McKenna on TV if you are able to view the broadcast. This process can reduce or eliminate any strong, defeatist feelings, beliefs, emotions, as it can physical symptoms.

While tapping, you must continue thinking about your problem throughout the whole sequence.

Close your eyes and think about your problem. On a scale of 0 – 10, 0 being nothing and 10 being the worst it could ever be, where is your problem?

Still thinking about the problem, take two fingers of either hand and tap firmly 10x above one of your eyebrows at the inner end nearest your nose.

Tap the outside end of your eye 10x.

Now tap under that eye 10x.

Tap under your nose 10x.

10x under your bottom lip.

Now tap under your collar bone 10x, just below the V notch.

As you continue to think about your problem, tap under your armpit 10x.

Tap on the karate chop side of your other hand.

Tap on the back of your other hand just below the knuckles of your ring finger and little finger and keep doing so. While doing so, open your eyes, then close them. The following eye movements are connected to various brain functions.

Keep tapping. Open your eyes, look down to the left, then center, then right.

Keep tapping and as you do so, rotate your eyes 360 degrees anti-clockwise, then 360 degrees clockwise.

Still thinking about the problem, hum the first few lines of Happy Birthday or a favorite tune. This humming allows switching between the right brain hemisphere – left brain hemisphere – right brain hemisphere activity.

Next, count aloud from 1 – 9.

Repeat the first few lines of the tune.

Still thinking on the problem, close your eyes, tap 10x above your eye again and go through the previous routine.

Finally tap on the karate chop point again.

Where is your problem now on the scale of 0 – 10? You should have it down to a manageable level by the second go. If it hasn't reduced, go over the sequence again. It depends on how strong your problem was to start with, so it may need several attempts to reduce or completely eliminate it. Repeat as needed. You may get confused about what used to bother you.

Now I'll show you how to create a brilliant bodybuilding future with time line...

TIME LINE

Part of you that is curious may wonder about this exercise. Think of a time ahead where you can see yourself celebrating a success, holding aloft a trophy while you see and hear the champagne corks popping, see and hear your supporters cheering for you. When you imagine that kind of future, your subconscious is directed towards making it happen.

Devised by Tad James, another psychology pioneer, A *Time Line* is thought of as an imaginary line where events happen and even where the subconscious stores memories. This line stretches off in one direction to your future and in the opposite direction for your past. Examples of this would be when you say "I am looking forward to seeing you," or "I'll put this problem behind me."

There are two parts to this exercise. But first, how do you represent time? Think about something you do every day, if it's related to bodybuilding so much the better. Let's say you are mixing a weight gain and protein drink because you gain weight too slowly. As you see yourself doing the activity tomorrow, notice the direction you are looking. Is your future in front, or is it to your left or right? Higher or lower? How far away?

Think about doing that task next week. Is the image further away, in front, behind, to the side, higher or lower? Stay with me on this. What about a week ago in the past, where are you doing the activity then?

Think about mixing the weight gain and protein drink a month in the future. Is the image further away or closer? More in front or behind? More to one side or another? How about a month ago?

You can go on imagining the same activity three, six, twelve months in the future. Where is the picture in your mind?

Imagine all these scenes of you mixing the drink are joined together by a line, as if you were connecting them as dots inside your mind. This is how you subconsciously see time, your Time Line.

The second part of this exercise is creating your bodybuilding future to live into. Project yourself several months into your future, maybe winning a competition having put on muscle weight, or you have reached a goal. Everything has gone well, you've improved, you're more confident , you're more knowledgeable. You have achievements in your life outside bodybuilding.

Be curious about your future. Form an image of that ideal scene of everything you wish to happen in your future. It can be real or symbolic. See yourself there, happy and successful. Make the image big, bright, colorful, close up and feel how good you will feel the sparkle.

Now fill in the steps along the way to this ideal scene. Make a smaller image and place it a few weeks, or months, before this final big picture. Keep doing this until you have a succession of images connecting the present to your ideal future so that they get bigger each time, with good things happening along the way.

Look at those pictures you have created as stepping stones and imagine floating up out of your body and into each picture, spending a few moments living in each to absorb the positive experiences.

When you reach that final image, really get into the feeling of achievement as you discover yourself already there.

Finally return to the present and look along your future Time Line. Have confidence in the knowledge that it is a map for your subconscious to bring fulfillment to the future you have created, evolving your approach to exercise and nutrition and a positive overall lifestyle.

Next, let's talk about pain control...

PAIN CONTROL

Tom Watson

No medical claims are expressed or implied here. You must only use these pain control techniques when you know the cause of your pain. Whatever the results you get, please continue to take any action or medication prescribed by your health practitioner.

You deal with pain on a daily basis in the gym. There can often be risks of injuring yourself by putting unnecessary stress on your body, seeing how much weight you can lift for ego's sake. Pain means there is something wrong. If there is something wrong, you must seek medical assistance.

If you suffer pain or discomfort in any part of your body, just fifteen minutes of this exercise can make it disappear or diminish it significantly. Using the power of their mind, most people who have given this exercise a go reduced their pain by up to 80%.

A closed eye process is best so learn the method first or have someone read it to you. It's a simple exercise, the purpose is to look at pain from a different perspective so you are looking beyond the pain. To your surprise you can get rid of it. Want it to happen, expect it to happen, allow it to happen. The power of your mind is powerful enough.

Get yourself relaxed somewhere you won't be distracted. Without judging if you are doing it right, dismiss your rational mind and locate exactly the condition in your body you are suffering from. Now describe the pain.

How big is it? How long, thick, wide? What shape is it? A cube, flat, rectangle, square, triangle, jagged? Is it dull or sharp?

Just keep focusing on the sensation and describe exactly how it feels. Pressing, pounding, pulsating, tearing, tingling, stretching?

Does it have a color? A smell? A weight? If you're not sure, make it up.

Does it move?

Is there a temperature?

Now you have the location, shape and sensation of the condition, are you willing to let this condition go?

I want you to go inside your body and take the thing out. You can read that sentence again. Just imagine that you are reaching inside and taking it out.

With your eyes still closed, imagine it in your hands. How big is it? What color is it now? What shape? Is it hard or can you manipulate it? Can you roll it up into a ball? Go on, play with your condition. Toss it up into the air a few times, then throw it away saying "goodbye" or "I no longer want this."

Look inside. How are your symptoms now?

Let's focus on it again. Has it moved? How big is it? Smaller than before? What color? What shape? The same or changed?

Again, reach in and take any more out of your body. Go ahead. How does it feel? Can you bend it?

Drop it to the floor. Does it make a noise? Does it break into pieces? Pick it up and roll it into a ball again. Tell yourself you no longer want it and throw it away.

How are your symptoms now? You can repeat the process as often as you need. As you reduce or eliminate the condition, you become mentally stronger.

Gently center back into your body and slowly open your eyes. Be still a moment.

That exercise can also be used on emotional issues such as anger, grief and fear.

***

I'd like to talk about *Noesitherapy* – healing by thinking and here credit the founder Dr Angel Escudero, a surgeon in Valencia, Spain. He has been investigated by medical experts who have praised his methods. He has lectured to the medical profession and he has been featured on a number of TV broadcasts around the globe. Dr Jonathan Royle who taught this, uses Noesitherapy as part of his Complete Mind Therapy.

The theory behind Noesitherapy stems from the fight or flight response. Back in time, the caveman developed the fight or flight response which is basically the way adrenaline flows through your body. The muscles become strengthened which means you can fight more vigorously, or run away faster. Our caveman was constantly on full alert, especially when out hunting. He would fight an opponent or an animal, but there would still be fear. His mouth would go dry, muscles would tense and he would have extra strength due to the physiology of his body. When he defeated his foe or killed the animal, he would sigh with relief.

If he met a large animal that wanted him for its dinner, then flight would be the action. If he managed to get away, he sighed with relief and notice again, his mouth was dry. That's the key! After any stress is over, saliva returns to a dry mouth. We also sigh and the muscles relax. I'll not get involved here with the other physical signs of heart beat, sweating, blood pressure, digestion, which has come from thousands of years of conditioning in humans, who now live in a different age, just remember the saliva.

It's the apprehension, fear or expectancy of feeling pain that makes pain hurt or exist at all. You can finish a DIY task and go to the sink to wash your hands and see blood. You did not notice when the cut happened as your mind was somewhere else. The moment you see the blood, the cut starts stinging and funnily enough, bleeds more.

If you're injured and you are told you have to live with a certain amount of pain, then being able to re frame your mind so there's no pain, maybe just a little discomfort, makes the pain bearable.

Use the 0 – 10 scale to judge how much pain you are experiencing.

Besides breathing deeply, your body is conditioned to relax with saliva. Use the idea of a lemon to get saliva working in your mouth. Let's suppose you have injured your right elbow by seeing how much weight you could lift with a dumbbell for your ego's sake. Imagine you're eating a tangy, juicy lemon and get the saliva on your tongue. This part is going to sound daft. Bare with me. Say to yourself aloud if you can while the saliva is on your tongue, "my right elbow is now completely anesthetized," which you say three times. If you're in a public place you can say it to yourself. Why three times? The concept behind that is the first time your subconscious may ignore the conscious command as it is busy with other tasks. The second time the subconscious realizes you are there and listens out and the third time the subconscious realizes it is true and activates in a way that is right for you. Besides, Dr Escudero does it with his patients and he then carries out amputations.

Take a nice, deep, relaxing breath. Imagine your right elbow has gone cold, it's like a lump of meat from the freezer. There's no discomfort to concern you. In a moment you can swallow the saliva, just say a few affirmations to yourself, such as "I an without discomfort." You can turn pain off like a switch. Where is the pain now on the 0 – 10 scale?

***

There are many studies that have been carried out using hypnosis for pain relief and even performing surgery. One of the basic methods for using hypnosis for this is *Glove Anesthesia.*

It's tough if you find yourself unable to train through an injury. You can do nothing, or use your time wisely. List the things you can do, perhaps studying a bodybuilding DVD, reading, performing any exercise you can do, even if it's sat on an exercise bike with your arm in a sling.

Find a comfortable, quiet place where you will not be disturbed. Close your eyes, get yourself more relaxed and focus on your breathing. Let it be steady, deep and slow. Imagine relaxing all the muscles in your body from the top of your head, down, one muscle group at a time. Use your awareness and focus on those muscles and think the words "soft and relaxed," as you imagine them melting, softening into relaxation.

Imagine you are in a favorite place, somewhere you feel safe and relaxed. Imagine you can see all the sights of that place, hear all the pleasant sounds, feel the good feelings you would feel. Take your time.

Using your self-talk, tell yourself you have the power and ability to be in control of any sensations in your body. Because you do! Accept you are in control of the unlimited power of your mind. You can send numbing sensations into any part of your body. Encourage and empower yourself. Believe in the power of your mind.

Imagine that those words of power and belief are being delivered to the deepest parts of your mind and are being accepted on every level of your body and mind.

Concentrate now on your dominant hand. As you focus on that, really notice all the tiny sensations within it. Begin to imagine that your dominant hand is now free of all feeling, perhaps as it would be if it became encased in ice. Truly imagine this. As you continue to place your attention on your hand, allow it to lose all feeling.

Tell yourself your hand is becoming numb, no feeling at all. Your hand has gone to sleep. Be aware of all those unusual sensations that are there in your hand as you concentrate on it. Tell yourself that every breath you take causes your hand to become more numb until you cannot feel your hand at all, you just cannot feel your hand, no feeling at all.

Now you can transfer this numbness to any part of your body that is feeling pain. So when you are sure you have developed the correct level of numbness in your hand, you can move it to the part of your body you want to feel numb.

That's it! You can transfer the numbness when you raise your dominant hand and touch the part you want to have treated. You can imagine that part of your body being filled with a color which is spreading into the area, creating numbness and bringing recovery. Imagine all the sensations of numbness ate being transferred from your hand into that injured part of your body, making it better.

Give yourself a time limit that this will last for, you don't want the numbness to last a lifetime. Make sure you set a time limit when your anesthesia will end. When you have transferred that soothing, healing numbness, the area becomes better and better. Imagine you are experiencing relief in the area.

When you have a good state and are feeling good, say the word "anesthesia." Your mind can focus on the right *intention and resources to do this again. Trust that each time you do Glove Anesthesia it has a great effect on enhancing your control over your self-treatment which will be more powerful and profound.*

***

Run video in your head of exercising. This keeps your mind focused and positive. Your mind stores what you have experienced and what you have thought, the same way. This is perfect for mental training.

If you over-train, you feel lethargic, tired, even ill. If you feel pain or undue stiffness, get it looked at. No matter how confident you are, injuries do plant doubts in your mind which is why the mental side of recovery is so important. Now it's important for me to mark this next distinction for you – you are not injured anymore! You are in a state of recovery!

Be careful what you eat...

ALLERGIES

"All problems were once solutions."
Milton Erickson

Allergies are quite common and can be caused by prolonged exposure to a particular food you eat. Almost everything we eat these days is full of harmful bacteria or chemicals and even fresh food can be degraded by the packaging it is wrapped in.

The range of food-related allergens which have been tested by *muscle testing* is quite surprising. B vitamins, amino acids, dairy products, citrus fruits, some minerals and wheat. While the symptoms for reactions following exposure to these can be aches, bloating, diarrhea, dizziness, raised temperature and brain fog.

A for finding allergies, food deficiencies or an excess of substances consumed or used by you comes from

Applied Kinesiology. This allows someone to to identify allergens, both from food environmental factors that are harmful to your body. If the substance is harmful, muscles in your body instantly become weak when pressure is applied to them.

There are a number of minor preliminaries to Muscle Testing. Be hydrated. Have no caffeine, stimulants or alcohol before testing. Remove any jewelry. It is best to test standing, but if sat down, keep your legs uncrossed.

Place one finger at your naval to earth your body and gently rub just below your collar bone, about 2cm either side of the 'V' notch for a minute or two. This is K27 used in acupuncture.

Close your eyes and place your arm out to the side, horizontal with the ground, palm down. With the help of a friend, who will place one hand on your shoulder and with their other hand, place two of their fingers on your wrist, then apply slight pressure down for about two seconds while you resist and hold your arm steady to determine arm strength. As your friend does this, you will be establishing a 'yes' or 'no' response by repeating a true or false statement, e.g. "my name is Bill."

Now perform the intolerance test, While holding your arm out to the side as before, hold the substance you wish to test at your stomach. Some items may have to be placed in a glass container. Never use plastic. Just before your friend applies two-finger pressure to your wrist, ask "is this good for me?" Then test.

If you are testing supplements, ask, "do I need to take this?" or "is this good for me?"

Kinesiology is the study of human movement, while Applied Kinesiology is an alternative method of medical diagnosis. Originated in the 1960s by Dr John Good heart as a system for obtaining feedback in order to examine the functioning of the human body. He found that muscles instantly became weak when the body is exposed to harmful substances. If the body is in balance, the muscles remain strong and firm.

Stay motivated with a bodybuilding scrap book...

BODYBUILDING
SCRAP BOOK

*"Peak performance from various fields maintain
their childlike qualities!"*
Lars Eric Unestahl

Anyone wishing to invest time in bodybuilding is strongly advised to learn as much as they can about the sport. Read books and magazines, watch films, talk to people involved. Take clippings, pictures, photos or photo copies. Collect brochures of anything to bring into your bodybuilding life, events, symbols, anything that gives you motivation and support. Use training logs to keep an account of your bodybuilding activities.

Every time you look at them, they remind you of your goals yet to achieve, your role models, places you would like to train, equipment you would like to own.

Use bodybuilding bookmarks, drink from a bodybuilding mug, dream in bodybuilding bedding.

Do the same with a video/DVD scrapbook. Watch the top stars, study what works for them. Pay close attention and watch everything you can about what the champions do.

Here's how to analyze yourself. Buy, rent or borrow a DVD camera. Get a tripod, manually focus on where you will train or practice posing and film yourself. Review the film. You may be surprised. I guarantee as you watch yourself, you will notice things about your technique that you did not realize you were doing and you may be able to uncover information of what's clearly been a blind spot in your awareness.

Keep items about your home or room that act as powerful anchors. Look at and handle them frequently. Use regular rehearsal time to look, hear and feel those things. Give yourself a sensory-rich experience. Concentration and rehearsal brings in countless nerve impulses.

Going slightly further, it may be helpful to concentrate on a picture or an object. Study it while relaxing. Use it like a meditation session. When you notice your thoughts begin to wonder, return your full attention to your picture/object. This exercise will improve your ability to focus and give you awareness of where your mind drifts.

Learn from the legends. Get a picture of your hero in action and splice a photo of your head onto their body. Put it somewhere you can view it often. You may not have all your hero's qualities, but you're empowering your mind and stretching it beyond any limitations. Read the *Mirroring* chapter again, then copy and pretend until you become your own hero.

Cool down is almost upon us...

CONCLUSION

> *"Whether you think you can or think you can't,
> your probably right."*
>
> Henry Ford

I'm done. Being physically fit is only part of training these days. There's not a lot published on the psychology of bodybuilding, I hope this book has given you an insight. As you can see, mental and emotional strength are also required to create the best body. I've covered mind techniques that can change your bodybuilding outlook, not just now, but progressively for years to come.

This was written with bodybuilders in mind, however, many of the methods described are able to cross over into other areas of your life. As you become familiar with them, your energy and motivation will improve.

If you do nothing, what will happen? If you take responsibility to do something, what will happen?

Even a small change to your thinking will make a big difference. As you continue with this new way, you'll begin to realize how much you have changed. Don't look how far you have to go, rather how far you have come. As you have learned, the conscious mind can only think of one thing at a time, why not make it something positive. You can, can you not!

You can often be the last person to notice any changes. Keep an ear open for comments from friends and colleagues. Maybe you will hear them comment on how happy you have become lately or you're becoming more confident in all the things you do.

You should make this book important enough to return to it several times to get the results you need. Why not carry it in your kit bag. No single technique is a magic pill, but when you practice repeatedly, the techniques will become familiar. You may even find one an exciting and rewarding activity.

When I was learning to drive, I practiced again and again until I was confident enough to pass my test, just as drivers before me have done. All I needed was the confidence practice would bring. I didn't presume driving wouldn't work on my very first attempt. Please keep that in mind. If a method doesn't work for you on your first attempt, don't give up on it. Understand these tried and tested methods do work. They work beautifully.

Imagine staring into a mirror after training and honestly telling the person you see facing you, you have done your best. Feel the pride, feel the joy that has been created by your efforts. The delight you have created in your training, your coach, your family.

I sincerely hope you enjoy what has been presented here and I really want you to succeed, because by your success this book will be judged. Have fun and enjoy your bodybuilding.

APPENDIX 1

Fundamentals of Bodybuilding for Competition

Introduction

The majority of people who weight train do so for non-competitive reasons, usually to enhance their fitness, appearance, or both. Bodybuilders the world over are motivated mostly by their desire to build the largest muscles they can gain. Many have the potential to develop their bodies, yet few are able to reach it, mostly due to psychological issues.

One thing to remember about bodybuilding is there is no need to get stressed about doing everything perfectly. There is no need to get stressed about anything. Offered is this book are a variety of mental training techniques you can do to provide drive and ambition and improve your physique so you can reach the goals and results you aim for over time. However, the key is always do something, no matter how small. Eventually you will astonish yourself.

If you have been training for some time, you may have considered entering a competition. In the majority of cases, most bodybuilders will first have to train regularly one to two years before they will develop sufficient mass to think about competing. When that time comes and a concrete decision has been made to compete in a specific contest, a scientifically structured preparation routine needs to be thought out thoroughly to bring you to the absolute peak of condition by competition day.

Muscle & Fat

Training must be intense enough to promote adaptation of size and strength. With a beginner, for a while there will be progress, however, at the more advanced stages, growth issues become more complex due to changes in physiology. As a bodybuilder gets bigger and stronger, the likelihood of over-training increases dramatically. Progress also slows down or comes to a halt altogether. The greater the demand imposed on your body through weight training affects your resources, your reserves and your recovery. The average person has the capacity to increase their strength by up to 300%, but their ability to recover from intense stresses imposed upon their body can only increase by about 50%. You therefore have to exercise self-control to make sure your body has time to recover and grow.

Gaining a top level physique is a slow business when growing pure muscle tissue. A 5 – 10 lb gain of pure muscle per year is a huge achievement. It may not sound much, but looked at over a period of several years, it becomes quite a lot of muscle. At the rate of 10lb of muscle a year for five years you would gain 50lb of pure muscle. Here's another way to look at it. If when you started bodybuilding you weighed 120lb and ten years later you hit the scales as 165lb, that breaks down to 4.5lb of muscle gained each year.

We are restricted in how thick a muscle can become. The longer a muscle is from it's origin to it's insertion, the thicker it can develop. But if the muscle is only one inch long, it will never get thicker than one inch. It's width will never exceed it's length. What is important is the length of the muscle in comparison to the bone it lives on. Does your bicep extend the full length of your humerus?

The criteria for judging contests include in addition to muscle mass, the absence of any body fat to emphasize muscle definition, symmetry or proportion development, overall appearance and posing.

Consider professional bodybuilders and see how they are able to reach a peak consistently from contest to contest. You have to assess your existing condition to give yourself adequate time to develop as much muscle mass as possible, uniformly, over your entire body through training and diet, so you will peak by a per-determined date, with overall body fat being as little as 3 – 6%.

The time needed to prepare will depend on your existing body fat ratios. The leaner you are when you start contest preparation then the less time will be required. Remember, it is difficult to build muscle and lose fat simultaneously. When dieting too severely coupled with over-training, will lead to muscle loss. Even on the most severe diet regime, the maximum body fat you can safely lose is 3lb a week, so you can lose 18lb in six weeks. If you attempt to lose fat too fast, you can lose muscle also. Losing 2lb of fat a week is more practical and reduces the likelihood of losing any muscle. It is best to reach a peak and maintain it rather than continue to diet.

Assessing how much of your body is fat can be done in a number of ways. Hydro-static weighing is expensive while skin pinch calipers are simple to use but not so accurate. The easiest and least expensive way is to use a mirror. Many bodybuilders are mirror shy so spend little time studying their reflection. You need to practice the technical aspects of your posing, co-ordination and analyze details of your appearance. Do your chest muscles have a squared off look? Is the area around your naval tight? Can you grab an inch or more of skin around your lower back on either side of your spine just above your hips? If so, you will probably need around ten weeks of dieting and training to get sufficiently ripped. You could also make a DVD of your routine to further analyze and upgrade your presentation.

Five to six weeks should be dedicated to contest preparation. More than ten to twelve weeks will become draining and taxing on both your mind and body. Your final week should be spent practicing posing and relaxing a little so you feel like you can finish fresh and strong on contest day.

A favored training formula used before contests should include weight training that progressively declines in intensity the final two weeks leading up to your contest and some aerobic activity that increases in duration and frequency the last four to six weeks before the contest.

At the start of the contest preparation your weight training sessions should be very intense and the aerobic activity be of short duration. Cycling six to ten miles a day at a slow pace once or twice a week combined with or alternating with jogging one and a half to two miles should be adequate. As contest time gets nearer, removing body fat becomes an ever increasing issue and the intensity of weight training sessions will decrease as aerobic activity increases, until cycling at least twice a week for thirty to forty five minutes and running three or more miles on alternate days. Jogging a mile will burn around 100 – 120 calories or roughly 15 calories a minute while cycling at a moderate pace, say between 8 – 12 mph burns about 8 calories a minute.

Competition

It takes a long time, with discipline and the dedication of hard training and dieting to build a champion physique. Have you also considered the importance of effective posing and preparation. To pose in your most self-flattering and artistic manner possible will bring value to your appearance, so you must become proficient at all the aspects of posing and be comfortable at presenting them in a polished stage performance.

Wear an appropriate posing costume. If you have a long torso your trunks should be high on the waist. If you are short, then your trunks should be cut lower to generate a more elongated appearance. If your thighs are short, then your trunks should be cut higher and for longer legs, your trunks should be cut lower. If you have dark skin or a dark bronzed skin tone, your costume should range from a pale yellow to a dark red, while lighter skin tones are better with earth colors in shades such as browns and greens and avoid flesh colors completely.

The style of your posing must serve as an expression of your physical attributes while at the same time convey your personality. Once you have chosen seven or eight basic posses by kneeling, striding, twisting, all performed effortlessly and gracefully.

Think about how you conduct yourself at a contest. How do you behave while signing in? During per-judging? During the show and even when leaving the premises? Your actions will have an affect on the overall view of you as an individual and advance your reputation when the next contest comes around.

APPENDIX 2

Self-Hypnosis for Bodybuilding

Introduction

Sports hypnosis can be a vital psychological tool that can assist sports people to get the best out of themselves in training and in competition. It helps them to create a powerful vision that will improve their abilities, so they can achieve the wishes they long for to the exclusion of all other critical, negative and distracting thoughts which may create doubt in any ability.

Your inner mind holds the memory of everything you have ever witnessed or experienced. Your inner mind does not distinguish between experiences that are imagined or that are real. When you vividly imagine an experience, neurologically it has already taken place. Your goal might be to win a regional tournament. Create a vivid picture in your mind of what the winning experience might be like. What it feels like to be standing on the stage, the audience showing applause, feeling the blood pump through your veins and that thrill as a heavy medal is hung around your neck.

When you imagine that in vivid detail you are exposing it to your inner mind as effectively as if you were actually standing on the stage with the audience applauding as that medal is hung around your neck. Repeat this vividly and consistently with self-hypnosis and soon you start doing what a winner does, take the actions of a winner and living the way a winner lives.

When a sportsperson is in the relaxed, receptive state hypnosis brings, the critical faculties of the conscious mind are suspended, enabling the person to become receptive to positive suggestions. They can see themselves successfully executing skills, movements and other sports experiences they train for.

Even if someone is limited in their physical activity because of injury, they can remain positive and overcome any negative mindset, maintain their sense of purpose, keep passion for their sport alive and overcome distress.

Hypnosis

To begin, there are many myths about hypnosis, often undeserved which I should clear up. It is not magical, nor does it give someone magic powers. It cannot turn you into Superman otherwise we would all be flying around. You cannot get stuck in hypnosis. You do not place yourself under another persons power who will then take control of you. You cannot become possessed. You cannot be made to do something which is against your moral code. You do not leave your body. You do not lose your mind.

Let me reassure you, hypnosis is a natural state of mind which can be used as an efficient psychological tool for a body builder to reach full potential. Self-hypnosis can be a wonderful vehicle to get you into the performance zone.

Those easiest to hypnotize have the strongest, most creative minds with the greatest ability to use their concentration, imagination and intelligence. Very few people are not able to get into a hypnotic state and there is usually a reason. Epilepsy can create difficulty to focus, the really mentally subnormal, senility and those suffering alcohol or drug abuse.

Hollywood and the media thrive on drama and many stories in books and on film are the child of fertile imaginations of their writers. Victims lose control of their minds from the power of the evil hypnotist to heighten any tension in the story line. Those authors and script writers have probably been influenced by a previous writers mistaken idea of what hypnosis is all about.

More misunderstandings come from stage shows where, I must stress here, the participants are in full agreement to the suggestions they are given. Those people on stage are volunteers who are fully prepared to go along with the entertainment. And that is all it is, entertainment.

With clinical hypnosis I am not going to get you to bark like a dog, that's not going to get you to transform your body, or help you achieve your weightlifting goals. Hypnosis is a reliable, therapeutic method recognized by orthodox medicine.

Here you will discover how to help yourself achieve success in bodybuilding. Surprisingly you have been in hypnotic trances many times before, although you may not have realized. A regular journey, to the gym for example, when you don't remember getting there. Don't worry about anything like that though, your subconscious is on constant duty making sure you are safe. As soon as conscious attention is needed, your subconscious gets you there instantly.

How about reading a book when you realize you haven't noticed a single word because your mind has been in some other place. Or you're watching a film and you don't hear someone talking to you until they start shouting to get your attention, because you have been absorbed with the story on the screen. These are all forms of trance which happen to you every day. The examples show you were focused, however on something else.

Some clients think they failed to go under as nothing more than extreme relaxation took place. They knew they could move or open their eyes if they wanted to, they were just too comfortable to be bothered. That is what hypnosis can be like for some people. The best way to describe what you may experience, is remember how you feel just moments before actual sleep occurs, or moments before you wake up fully. At that moment you pass through a state very similar to hypnosis.

Here are some of the sensations you may experience, it is different for everybody:

Extremely relaxed
Floaty
Tingling in your hands or features
Feeling either light or heavy
More awareness, senses heightened
Warmth or cold
Stress free

Preparation

I'm going to teach you a preparation routine which I would like you to practice. This has been adapted from a self-hypnosis script by Terence Watts of Hypnosense who has many more scripts and learning material available on his website. Do it with your eyes open a few times so you can read yourself through it, it's easy to remember.

Make sure you won't be disturbed for about ten minutes and visit the toilet before you begin. Sit comfortably. Some people prefer a straight-backed chair to an armchair. Have both your feet flat on the floor and your hands relaxed on your lap. There is a position where your head feels as if it has no weight, find that position where your head feels weightless so your head is exactly aligned over your body and your breathing is at it's best.

Exercise

Close your eyes and be aware of your breathing and imagine a feeling of ease and peace drifting down through your body relaxing every muscle. If you find that difficult, imagine how it would feel if your muscles were relaxed. Slow your breathing right down so that your breathing so gently, you wouldn't disturb a feather placed on your nose.

Don't force it. Relaxation comes in it's own time. After a while, you'll feel yourself becoming calmer, quieter, your mind as still as your body. It's even fine if you notice you're more aware than ever before. Stay with it.

And open your eyes when you are ready. How was that? You can actually go into hypnosis with that simple routine. You may have been surprised at just how easy images can form.

Visualization

You should practice and become good at visualization as it will lead you to success in your aims and goals. Some people think they cannot visualize anything as they can't see pictures in their mind's eye. You don't have to see something exactly as if you were looking at a photograph. For you, there may be a specific sound, tactile feeling, even a smell that can create the moment you want rather than just seeing it. Try this. Remember a short journey you have done today. Something as simple as going from your front door to your living room. Imagine in your mind starting out and finishing the journey. Whatever it was, that's a visualization for you.

Effective visualization practice should use more of your senses than just visual imagery. This way your other senses can be strengthened. Imagine what coffee smells like? How about fresh cut grass? Can you imagine hearing weights being loaded onto a barbell? What does your hair feel like? Don't touch it, imagine it. You may be more aware of another sense than vision.

Once you get used to it, you'll soon be able to imagine every smell you can think of, any sound you have ever heard, any texture you have felt. Practice, smell things, feel things, listen to sounds and once you have your visualization set, you need to ensure that your every day beliefs are in line with what you want to achieve. Use effective affirmations by making them bold, clear, positive, stated in the present tense.

Exercise

Find somewhere comfortable to sit where you won't be disturbed for twenty minutes or so. Put to one side any problems you are having to deal with, they will still be there when you come back. In fact, after some mental work, you may be able to deal with them more efficiently. One easy trick is to visualize a kit bag where you can place all your mental and emotional troubles until you have time to sort them out.

Go through the preparation routine as before and when you are ready, recall some ordinary event that's happened in the last day or so. Remember your senses. How did it look? How did it sound? How did it feel? How did it taste or smell?

With practice, your memories will become more detailed. These images, when used in hypnosis, provide as edge to creating maximum success, as you shall see.

Let's get into self-hypnosis...

Self-Hypnosis

You should now be comfortable with the preparation and visual routines as I'm going to explain to you a three-part routine for getting into the hypnotic state.

But first, how do you come out of self-hypnosis? Simply finish the session by telling yourself to do so. Tell yourself you will be wide awake and alert, feeling fine on the count of five then count yourself up from one to five and open your eyes. Practice that a few times.

Part 1
Close your eyes. Bring to mind a special day that you have had, if it's related to bodybuilding so much the better. Bring all of your senses in, remembering what you saw, what you heard, what you felt, even what you smelt or tasted if they are relevant. Notice how the memory starts, remember it and store it in your mind, you will use it later.

Make everything real in your mind and keep focused until you can almost re-live one or more of those senses. It will often be the visual one, but don't let it concern you if you don't get it exact, it takes practice. As long as you have an awareness something is there is fine enough. Allow it to happen rather than force it to happen.

Part 2

With your eyes closed, imagine you are breathing peace into every cell of your body, each and every fiber of your being. And with every exhalation, you are letting go of any tension. Let each and every muscle from your head to your toes go limp as you exhale and repeat the word "relax." After half a dozen or so breaths, let yourself imagine you are drifting further down and you are becoming more relaxed, more than you have ever been. If you feel yourself floating up, just go with that.

Part 3

Remember in Part 1 storing the memory of a perfect day? You can use that now as a trigger for getting into self-hypnosis. This is best achieved after getting some practice with the first two parts. To use this trigger is very simple. After doing the preparation routine (it gets easier and quicker the more you practice) and once you are settled with using Part 2, bring your happy memory to mind and let it help you drift down into trance – it's that easy!

When you are ready, count yourself out.

I or You

There are countless ways to achieve self-hypnosis, the method I have shown you is just one. When you're in, read a prepared script or use a recording to give yourself your desires. It's best to work on one thing at a time.

It's usual for people to say "I will," or "I can," or "I'm going to…" This may be fine for you, but some people respond better by being told what to do, such as "you will," or "you can," or " you're going to…" It does not matter what you use, 'I or You' as long as long as you use the form that feels right for you. If you're unsure, make a script or recording using both versions to see which one you feel more comfortable with, just don't mix the two forms up together.

Reading a script can be just as good as making a recording once you get yourself into hypnosis. Have you ever been so absorbed in a book you lost all sense of time? Someone spoke to you and you didn't notice? That's hypnosis. Once your in hypnosis just tell yourself you will open your eyes and start reading following Part 3, read, then at the end of the script, close your eyes ready to count yourself back. For either script or recording, you may enjoy some quiet relaxation music playing in the background.

Now I'll show you how to use the state of hypnosis to achieve bodybuilding mastery.

Use

Let's look how to actually use self-hypnosis to achieve your goals and desires. Be sure you're now used to getting into and out of hypnosis, if you're not, your efforts will be wasted. I cannot repeat this enough, you must have a full grasp on how to do it. The direct suggestions you will give yourself have to be compounded, so practice until it is so ingrained it will all be automatic.

You will always be aware of sounds as you are not asleep, so simply relax. If anything noisy happens outside, you are covered. Any sounds you hear will not affect or disturb you, in fact, you can actually use any sounds to deepen the trance. For example if there is heavy traffic outside, just tell yourself that all the traffic noise will help you to become more comfortable, deeper relaxed.

Caution

At the start of the session always tell yourself you will awake immediately if your full attention is needed for any emergency situation as a safety device. A further caution is not to drive or operate any machinery during your self-hypnosis session as it could slow down reflexes.

You can feel better, change habits, learn, block out pain and so much more. Just decide what goal you need. For setting your goals, there are four must rules that apply to every goal:

Plausible & Realistic

You nor I are magicians. If you are seventy years old you will not win Mr/Miss Olympia. If it's not possible without hypnosis, it's not possible with. However, hypnosis can get you to your highest standard possible.

Suitable for Personality

For your goal to succeed, it should reflect your personality. Although hypnosis allows people to behave in a way which can be different from their norm, that is only temporary, so it is no good for long-term goals. Select a goal which would not surprise a family member that you were doing it, then use hypnosis to speed up the process and become proficient at it.

Make it Clear

You need to know what it is that you want. Many people say "I want to be a winner." A winner at what? Your subconscious has the mind of a seven year old, it works only with uncomplicated, simple statements, not ambiguous ones. "I want to release six pounds of unwanted body fat," is a clear goal. That is achievable. Notice I wrote 'release' and not 'lose.' Lose is negative, nobody likes to lose anything.

Make it Positive

Think of what you want, not what you don't want. What you can do, not what you can't do. What you like, not what you don't like.

The Four Senses Test

You should apply at least four of your senses to any visualization of every goal. You should SEE yourself acting successfully, receiving a reward perhaps. HEAR something associated with it, applause maybe. FEEL something associated, how about the cool metal of that trophy in your hands and then SMELL or TASTE something there, celebratory Champagne perhaps.

Now turn all that into a living video, make it a rich, sense filled experience you can go over and over in your mind. As you practice using your senses, you will expand your conscious awareness.

It's best to work on one goal at a time, each goal can run into the next one as you progress. Working on one goal at a time makes it more likely for you to achieve it and is a lot easier than trying to remember a jumble of scenarios.

Get yourself into hypnosis and don't hurry it. Once there, play your video in your mind three, four, five times and let yourself feel the excitement of this adventure each time. That's an emotional reward for yourself and is an important part of the success plan, so make it your reality.

Each time you do self-hypnosis, you will do it better than the time before. Want it to happen, let it happen.

You now have the skills to improve your bodybuilding. Did you enjoy that?

Conclusion

That's all there is to it. There is far, far more to the art of hypnosis than I have covered here. There are many books, DVDs, courses on this fascinating subject and it's always good to compare more than one person's view on the subject.

Enjoy your bodybuilding.

Disclaimer

The author, Paul M Maher will not be held responsible for any accident or misadventure arising from the improper use of information laid out in this book. This book is written specifically for someone to learn self-hypnosis, not as tuition to hypnotize others.

If you enjoyed reading Bodybuilding Mind please write a review on Amazon. Say what you liked about it, if it helped you in any way and anything else you would have liked to have read. Thanks.

BIBLIOGRAPHY

Bolstad, Dr Richard., Resolve.

Callahan, Dr Roger., Tapping The Healer Within.

Court, Martyn., The Winning Mindset.

Eason, Adam., The Secrets of Self-Hypnosis.

Edgette, John H & Rowan, Tim., Winning The Mind Game.

Hodgson, David., The Buzz.

Lazarus, Jeremy., Ahead of the Game.

Liggett, Donald R., Sports Hypnosis.

Mack, Garry with Casstevens, David., Mind Gym.

McKenna, Paul., Change Your Life in Seven Days.

Mycoe, Stephen., Unlimited Sports Success.

Oswald, Yvonne., Every Word Has Power.

Robbins, Anthony., Awaken the Giant Within.

Robbins Blair, Forbes., Instant Self-Hypnosis.

Royle, Dr Jonathan., Confessions of a Hyptotist.

Waterfield, Robin., Hidden Depths.

Other Books by the Author

Cricket Mind

Soccer Mind

Tennis Mind